How to get the most out of your accountant

HOW TO GET THE MOST OUT OF YOUR ACCOUNTANT

J. L. Spencer, FCA

MERCURY

First published in 1992
by Mercury Books
Gold Arrow Publications Limited
862 Garratt Lane, London SW17 0NB

Cartoons by Ken Pyne

Set in Palatino by TecSet Limited
Printed and bound in Great Britain by
Mackays of Chatham, PLC, Chatham, Kent

British Library Cataloguing in Publication Data is available

ISBN 1–85252–106–6

Contents

Acknowledgements   vi
Introduction   vii

1   Why have an accountant? – And how to
    choose one   1
2   Self employment   10
3   Limited company audits   39
4   Restructuring your business   50
5   Buying another business   55
6   Being bought out   65
7   Franchising   69
8   Seeking management consultancy   74
9   Assistance for meetings with a tax inspector   81
10 Going for broke   93
11 For those on PAYE who have tax queries   97
12 Employing others   103
13 Financial services   106
14 Getting a mortgage   120
15 Other tax and trust advice   126
16 If you have doubts about your present
    accountant   132
17 What happens when you change accountants   140

Index   146

Acknowledgements

Although I have been involved in many thousands of client, and other, meetings and indeed lecture and train for companies on running meetings, this book is the product of more than the experiences of my own client base. Many others have assisted or offered material from their own client bases and I offer a collective thank you to these colleagues.

A number of people have offered special assistance and I would like to acknowledge these individually, with no discourtesy meant to anyone not mentioned; Adrian Pruss, my long-standing partner in management consultancy and training who assisted with the material for Chapters 4, 5, 6 and 8; Paul Benton, Group Controller of Barclays Life Assurance Co Ltd, who assisted with the material for Chapters 13 and 14; and Philippa Stedman, ACA, tax specialist, for assistance with Chapter 15.

None of these people are in any way responsible for any of the opinions and suggestions given in this book, responsibility for which must remain with me.

Introduction

Many people feel ill at ease when seeing professionals; accountants, doctors, solicitors and so on. Part of the problem is that they don't know how to prepare for meetings in a way that will give them confidence. Many first meetings are an abortive waste of everyone's time because the client simply does not know what to bring with them, what will be discussed, what an accountant can do for them, or how an accountant works.

The various sections of this book contain specific advice to assist in preparing for meetings with an accountant in each of the main situations you are likely to need one. The book also looks at when to engage one, how to choose one and, if necessary, how to change to another. The advice varies, of course, according to the situation. However, there are certain general points to be made which will help to save time – and therefore reduce fees – and which will help meetings to be more effective and satisfying for both you and your accountant.

Firstly, you should be sure that you know precisely what you want from the meeting. Ask yourself the questions:

- What do I want the result of this meeting to be – advice, a decision, an action or some other outcome?
- Is a meeting necessary or could this matter be dealt with more effectively by telephone, or in a letter?

A meeting with a specific, well thought out, reason has more chance of succeeding and it will run more efficiently. This is not to say that you will have considered every possibility; you may be surprised by suggestions or input from the accountant – indeed that is part of the point of having the meeting. However, if properly briefed, the accountant will have some idea of the 'target' for the meeting and between the two of you the meeting should be very cost effective.

It is important to telephone, or write to, your accountant ahead of the meeting and briefly outline the purpose of the meeting; your accountant will then be able to prepare his or her notes and obtain any necessary information – references, sections from Taxes Acts, Companies Acts and so on. Your accountant should be positively responsive to this approach and may even suggest to you other papers or information that you had not thought to bring, but which may be necessary.

You should ensure that any documents required are brought to the meeting; they should be arranged in an order that you are familiar with so that time is not wasted constantly shuffling through files, briefcases and so on to find particular sheets of paper. A half-hour of pre-preparation in the office or at home can save as much, or more, wasted 'shuffling' time enabling you and your accountant to stay focused on the issues. You will feel less ill at ease in the situation if you are familiar with your own paperwork, and remember also that you will perhaps be saving several tens of pounds in accountant's fees for time spent.

If you are concerned about the fees then telephone the accountant and ask what rate will be charged for a consultation of a given length of time. Basically, accountants charge at an hourly rate and will be pleased to discuss the basis of their charges with you. Of course it is not always possible to give a final quotation for a set assignment since there will be factors unknown prior to the meeting. Also, the accountant may have to call on other experts on your behalf, or may have to do further work, which will not necessarily be predictable at the outset. However, a simple question such as 'I want to consult you for one hour on a matter of personal taxation and I would like to know how much you will charge for that' should produce a reasonable quotation, subject to these other points. To this extent, at least, shopping for accountancy services should be no different from shopping at the High Street stores; you are entitled to know what price you are paying for the service before you go to the checkout.

A further important point: plan enough time for the meeting. Do not push yourself or your accountant to an unreasonable time limit. You should never feel pressured to finish a meeting prematurely or, worse still, have to go back for a second meeting just because you have had to go off to another appointment, golf game, the races or whatever. That said, some sort of anticipated time limit is important as it helps to concentrate the efforts of both you and your accountant; not allowing too many irrelevancies to creep in.

All this said, you must be reasonably flexible as you might not yet know the scope of your own enquiries (or you wouldn't be engaging an accountant) and the accountant clearly does not know fully what is going to be expected of him or her until you arrive. Let there be give and take on both sides.

The most amusing situation I ever sat through was a meeting with a client who – to his credit – had thought through his questions and noted them down. He sat opposite me with a written list of points which he proceeded to catalogue. After about five minutes I managed to get a word in and pointed out 'This is not what I thought we were going to be talking about. These are points that really should be discussed with a solicitor.' He looked at his watch, blushed very red and said 'Sorry, I thought for a moment there you *were* my solicitor; I remember now I'm seeing him this afternoon.' I suppose all professional offices look pretty much the same – and we had only met once before!

USING BRIEFCASE POINTS

To assist in pre-planning, each section of the book contains 'Briefcase Points': reminders either of things you should have considered before going to a meeting, or things you should take with you to the meeting ('in your briefcase'). The notes suggest that, although you might sometimes want to make a verbal presentation to your accountant (describing your business, for example), it is a good idea to write down your thoughts while preparing for the meeting – it is astonishing how many things you thought you knew about your own business become vague when you try to write them down and it will clarify many points that you may have consciously or unconsciously avoided thinking about.

1 Why have an accountant? – and how to choose one

Two experienced fishermen, Matthew and Mark, took an inexperienced companion, Luke, with them on a fishing trip. After a few hours they decided they were hungry but found they had left their lunchpacks on the shore. Matthew stepped over the side and walked across the lake surface to the beach, picked up the food and walked back to the boat. Luke watched, fascinated, but said nothing. Shortly afterwards they decided to get something to drink, and Mark stepped over the side of the boat, walked across the surface of the water and collected some drinks, then walked back to the boat. Luke was amazed. A few hours later the three ran out of bait, but they had further supplies in their bags on the shore. Luke volunteered to go, said a short prayer, took a deep breath and stepped over the side of the boat, immediately plunging into the water. Matthew and Mark quickly grabbed him and hauled him back into the boat, dripping wet. 'It is good that you have faith, of course,' they said, 'but it helps if you know where the rocks are.'

Your accountant is there to show you where the rocks are. In discussing the reasons for needing an accountant, and in deciding how to choose one, the first and

most obvious question might well be 'What is an accountant?'

This seems an easy question but in fact it is one of those to which everyone knows the answer until they are actually asked to give it. One frequently given response is 'An accountant is a person qualified to be an accountant.' While it is certainly true that somebody qualified in accountancy has the right to call themselves an accountant this is far short of the whole picture;

there are many people not qualified as accountants who use the title. A second answer frequently given is 'Someone who practises as an accountant.' This is getting closer to the truth; a practical and working definition of 'accountant' would appear to hinge on application. A person qualified to be an accountant but choosing to be, say, a pop musician might well have the option of calling themselves an accountant but would probably not do so. On the other hand somebody practising as an accountant, qualified or otherwise, would almost certainly use the term.

In this last point we discover something very important about the term 'accountant'. No qualifications are necessary for someone to call themselves an accountant; if the local butcher chooses to do accounts in his spare time, then he is an accountant. The distinction that must be drawn is between qualified and unqualified accountants. After having examined this we can look at the advantages of engaging accountants.

For the purpose of public practice, rather than specific industry, there are basically two qualifications at the 'top of the tree'; chartered accountants, i.e. members of the various bodies of the Institute of Chartered Accountants, and certified accountants, i.e. members of the Association of Certified and Corporate Accountants. Qualification with these bodies takes many years, several rigorous sets of examinations and proof of practical experience. For a public practising certificate there is a further requirement for proof of direct practical experience in certain fields.

Adequate for limited forms of practice, but lower in stature, are such qualifications as 'Accounting Technician' where there are similar rigorous examinations prior to qualification. There are many other qualified accountants, such as members of the Institute of Cost

and Management Accountants, but these are not qualifications directly relevant to public practice, indeed
their members who do choose to operate in public
practice either in their spare time or full-time could be
regarded as 'unqualified' for that purpose.

There are also a number of people who practise as
accountants who are trained only as bookkeepers, i.e.
they have training in double-entry bookkeeping but
very little wider knowledge or experience. Of the unqualified practitioners there are those who have, as
above, accountancy qualifications of a less relevant
type, those who have developed their accountancy
experience by working in accounts offices of companies,
those who have learnt to do specific types of bookkeeping and accountancy (perhaps dealing with their spouse's business records, and so on) and one or two who
merely offer to 'do the books' for colleagues or friends
based on bookkeeping they have seen in their
workplace.

If you are running a limited company then there is a
requirement for annual audit under the Companies
Acts. In this case you must appoint, at least as auditor, a
member of the Institute of Chartered Accountants or
the Association of Certified and Corporate Accountants. (There are also a number of people especially
licensed by the Department of Trade, but this is an
increasingly less relevant section.)

Apart from this audit situation, anyone, qualified or
unqualified, can act as accountant for a business, prepare accounts, submit them to the Inland Revenue for
approval, and so on. Alternatively, as there is no legal
requirement to appoint an accountant at all apart from
the audit requirement in limited companies, some businesses prepare their own records and make their own
submissions to such bodies as the Inland Revenue.

There is also of course the consideration of what form of business entity you should be operating in, i.e. partnership, limited company or other. This needs to be established at the beginning and the pros and cons of this question can be laid out by your accountant.

The two questions that arise therefore are:

- On what basis do you choose whether or not to appoint an accountant?
- How do you choose the accountant to appoint?

Deciding whether to appoint an accountant is obviously a question of requirements. There are certain reasons for engaging accountants where – generally speaking – no one would sensibly try to 'go it alone', such as the financial planning of an estate of considerable value where inheritance or gains taxes might be concerned. However, there are a number of people who feel content to prepare their own accounts and submit them to the Inland Revenue without engaging an accountant. Presumably this is on the basis that they have seen what a set of accounts look like, they are capable of adding up their own books and giving them to the Inland Revenue and, the Inland Revenue having passed them, they believe that all is well.

The point to remember is that you know all you know, but you don't know all other people know. Your accounts might well be overstating profit because you have failed to bring in some particular aspect of your business expenditure, not realising it was applicable. Since the Inland Revenue do not know of it they are happy to pass the accounts and for you, only ignorance is bliss. The question of how much you know as opposed to how much your accountant knows becomes

[5]

important at the time of starting a business when a great many important decisions have to be made: the appropriate year-end, when and how to notify the Inland Revenue that you have commenced trading, and so on.

I had one person come to my office who laid out his papers, saying that he had been in business for two years and that he had been handling his affairs very well up until then but felt that some of the letters from the Inland Revenue received recently were perhaps a little technical. As a result, he valued engaging me as his accountant to deal with them. As it turned out the reason the Inland Revenue's letters had become a bit difficult for him was because they had instituted a full investigation into his affairs, partly because of the manner in which he had declared his working from home and partly because he had failed to notify them appropriately within the correct time limits (and therefore rendered himself liable to interest and penalty charges). In any case he had appointed himself probably the worst possible year-end that he could have chosen; this has resulted in his permanently paying his taxes much earlier than would have been necessary with some forward planning.

In fact, I have yet to see a circumstance where anyone engaging an accountant has failed to recover the accountant's fees by perfectly legitimate tax and business planning and full consideration of the details of the business. At this stage I will nail my first set of colours to the mast and state that I believe all tax and accountancy advice and planning should be undertaken by accountants and that it is money well spent. The unfolding of the chapters ahead will allow the reader to determine whether or not that is a fair analysis.

With regards to who to appoint, it is only fair to start out by nailing a second set of colours to the mast and pointing out that I am a qualified chartered accountant. Qualified accountants are specifically trained to meet the requirements of their potential clients; they are also aware of where information has to be sought and of course they have the support of large institutes who are able to advise where their own expertise is limited.

That said, many unqualified accountants deal adequately with the requirements of their clients by building up a pool of expertise which – while not as wide as that of qualified accountants – is wide enough to deal with the scope of the work they become involved with. The problem can come when accountants are offered tempting jobs they are not qualified or able to take on, but take them on anyway. That said, this is applicable to both qualified and unqualified accountants, though the former do have the back-up of their institutes to assist them.

Probably the worst case of an unqualified accountant messing up a set of accounts, and certainly one with a touch of humour to it, was suffered by a client who came to me a few years ago. He was under investigation by the Inland Revenue because his accounts did not appear to be correct. It turned out that the Inland Revenue had been suspicious immediately on receiving the accounts because of the accountant's name; he was very well known to them as 'probably not terribly competent' being an ex-Inland Revenue officer!

Lastly, for this introductory chapter, there is one major criterion which assists those choosing qualified accountants. Their institutes have disciplinary bodies to whom the accountant can be reported in the event of inadequate service. Often a reasonable and justifiable threat to make such a report is itself enough to gain a proper response from an accountant. Unqualified accountants have no such governing bodies; the Inland Revenue will always take the view that any contract is between you and the accountant – not them and the accountant – and will not become involved in the debate so there is effectively no one for the client to complain to if the disciplinary bodies do not exist.

The question of cost is, of course, an important one. The absorbed overheads of accountants who make a full-time business of their profession can often mean that individual client charges are less for qualified accountants than for some unqualified accountants and there are certainly many cases where I – as a qualified chartered accountant – have taken over accounts from unqualifieds, and charged considerably less than my predecessors.

Having made a decision to appoint an accountant, qualified or unqualified, the choice of which accountant actually to appoint is very much a personal one. First, there has to be a certain amount of rapport between yourself and your accountant as clients very quickly find that they are placing in their accountant's trust something very akin to the health they place in a doctor's trust. Indeed for some clients it seems they are more relaxed discussing their health than they are their financial situation.

Secondly, the accountant should have at least some practical background knowledge of your particular industry, though for qualified accountants that is unlikely to be a difficulty. Certain industries require some sort of specialisation, such as the entertainment and film industries or the building industry, where there are particular regulations over and above normal accountancy and bookkeeping requirements.

Thirdly, there is the question of accessibility. Many clients do not need to see their accountant regularly, or indeed even from year to year, and are able to correspond and deal with matters by telephone; this is a perfectly satisfactory and valid way of dealing with matters providing it meets all the requirements of both parties. However, if you feel you will need to see your accountant regularly, or indeed you know that you are simply the sort of person who feels more at ease doing so, then it makes sense to appoint an accountant who can get to you easily or who you can easily visit. Extended travelling time is a waste of effort and money on your part and a valid reason for high accountancy fees on your accountant's part. Since accountants are not in particularly short supply anywhere in the country this, at least, should not be a problem.

Lastly, there is no better recommendation than that of somebody who is pleased with the accountant they have. While this may mean that you are engaging an accountant slightly out of your area it is certainly worth a great deal to know that there is already somebody you know and trust who is pleased with his work.

Briefcase Points

- Consider the advantages and disadvantages of both qualified and unqualified accountants.
- Do you require a qualified accountant for audit of a limited company?
- Can you get a recommendation from someone currently using an accountant?

2 Self-employment

By far the most common role an accountant plays is that of accountant and tax adviser to the self-employed. Most accountancy firms are general practices which by and large means they provide accountancy, audit and non-specialist taxation advice. From the self-employed person's point of view the accountant is very important because he or she is there to supplement the business, fulfilling the roles that an in-house finance department would deal with in a large business.

It is therefore very important that we look at the interaction between the accountant and the self-employed client and consider the many ways in which their relationship can be made more expedient. The 'Briefcase Points' are set out at the end of each sub-section of this chapter.

STARTING OUT

Your accountant will be familiar with the difficulties that have probably been experienced by many hundreds of clients similar to yourself, and before you even begin it may be advisable to talk to him about what the implications of self employment are. For many it is a dream come true; for others it is the realisation of their worst nightmares.

Self employment will affect not only you but your whole family. It will affect your social life adversely for some time, there will be periods of low income – even no income – and generally speaking you will work harder than as an employee because you will not only be the boss but also the tea-maker and all your own support services. They say that the self employed only have to work half the day – and they can pick their own 12 hours!

Your accountant will question you as to whether you have really considered your suitability for self employment in your chosen field. He or she will look at whether you have 'just a good idea' or a well thought out and integrated business plan involving not just your skills but drawing from skills that you may not have; for example you may be an excellent woodworker able to make intricate carved statues but you will make no money if you do not have the marketing of the product sorted out.

Your accountant can also advise as to the business vehicle you should start with; self employment (or partnership), a limited company or some other form of business organisation. If a limited company is the best vehicle then you will have to be aware of the duties and responsibilities of directors, which are onerous, of the statutory obligations under the Companies Acts and of the rights of shareholders. Your accountant can advise on these matters, many of which may have a bearing on your decision whether to incorporate or not.

An accountant can help you to formulate a business plan and possibly make appropriate presentations to the bank for initial finance. We will be looking at several of these particular areas in more detail in this chapter.

An accountant who is both experienced and wise can act as Devil's advocate and ask the questions that you are afraid to face. By the same token they should not be overly negative or unsupportive as you are going to need considerable energy and drive to succeed in your chosen field.

The balance will be a difficult one for both you and your accountant and from the word go you should see yourselves as something of a partnership.

That said, accountants' fees are high, as are most professional fees, and you should seek to minimise those costs by using your accountant to the most benefit in the shortest time. That is essentially what this section, and indeed this book, is about.

Briefcase Point

- Talk through your plans with your family before wasting time or effort on any further stages.

THE BUSINESS PLAN

Your accountant can help you to prepare your business plan which, in the first instance, will determine whether or not your proposal is a viable one. The plan must make clear both your personal and business ambitions and therefore you should have taken some time to consider this before speaking with the accountant.

The plan should record the history of the business, if it has one (it may be that you are changing the direction of an existing business or buying a new division, for instance), and should reflect its current financial state. Therefore you should have with you previous accounts (published or management), current existing cash flows and profit forecasts and recent and current bank statements.

The plan should include details of the principal people involved, their experience in that field of work and whether there are any known gaps in the management team. You should therefore bring to the meeting CVs in respect of key personnel.

There must have been some analysis of the market in which you are proposing to operate, and you should bring to the meeting details of any market research you have undertaken, details of your competitors, details of your own view of advertising needs and a statement of why you believe you can successfully break into and sustain a position in the market. Your accountant may wish to challenge some of your assumptions; believe it or not you will have made at least some of your decisions with rose-tinted glasses on! It is therefore important that you are able to support your statements with whatever evidence you have to hand. Bring with you your calculations of pricing policy including details of competitors' prices and details of your anticipated suppliers and any agreements you may have to enter into.

In order to prepare cash flow forecasts you will need to have organised credit terms with suppliers and have thought through what credit terms you are prepared to grant to your customers; bring these details with you also. If you have considered premises, machinery and staff requirements then have details of your calculations for those items to hand.

Very importantly, if you have identified that you require finance to start the business, bring with you any calculations in support of that and any information you may have regarding discussions with your bank, etc. Clearly this is an area where the accountant will be able to advise from personal connections with banks and other institutions. You will, however, have a certain track record with your own bankers and details of this may be vital if your accountant is to give you best advice. You can also obtain your accountant's advice on the best policy with regards to, say, an overdraft and/or loans.

Your accountant may be able to tell you about government schemes which act as incentives for you to start trading or to trade in certain areas. There are usually certain stipulations that your accountant can advise you of, and discuss whether or not you will be able to meet them.

The construction of this business plan will – more often than not – highlight at least some weaknesses in your thinking and occasionally show your proposals to be quite impractical; better to discover this now than in the bankruptcy court!

Briefcase Points

- History of the business, including previous published and management accounts.
- Current financial state of the business (including cash flow and profit forecasts).
- Recent and current bank statements.
- CVs of your partners, directors, main staff, etc. In addition, details of staff you think you will need.

- Market research results, if any, and details of advertising needs already identified.
- Pricing policy calculations and details of your competitors' prices.
- Credit terms agreed with suppliers.
- Credit terms you are likely to have to give your customers.
- Details of premises and equipment you already have, and those you are likely to need.
- Any correspondence or notes of meetings already held with banks, loan institutions, etc. regarding finance.

YOU AND THE INLAND REVENUE

Tax assessments for the self-employed are raised under a complex set of rules, particularly in the opening and closing years of a business. Advice is needed from the outset as to the best year-end to select for the business and possibly even the best time to cease activity, where choice exists. Your accountant will be able to examine your forecast of profits, or perhaps your profits for the opening few months, to ensure that you start off on the right foot. Selecting the right year-end can save a lot of tax permanently so choose the year-end with care; the partnership with your accountant should start as early as possible.

You might think that by starting your own business the question of whether you are self-employed or not is a very simple one, and indeed is just a matter of fact. However, the Inland Revenue could not pass up the chance to confuse the issue and they do have certain powers – which they are extending almost daily – to prevent people from calling themselves self-employed and forcing them into the PAYE system. Your accountant will be able to advise you as to whether or not the Inland Revenue are likely to take such a view in your case. If the Inland Revenue are not likely to accept your self-employed status it may save a lot of time and money to know that from the start.

In addition you may be able to save the Inland Revenue wasting their time and yours; if you present the facts poorly then the Inland Revenue may make a decision based on your statements which they may later have to reverse. Your accountant can advise you on the appropriate way to make the proper statements to avoid creating this confusion.

The self-employed are those who are taxed under Schedule D cases I or II of the Taxes Act. This refers to profits of trade or from practising a profession and the first question to ask is whether or not such a trade is being undertaken.

The 1954 Royal Commission on the taxation of profits and income summarised the criteria as the 'badges of trade'. A brief look at these will help you to decide whether your activities come under this category:

- Badge 1 relates to the goods being sold and whether or not they are being purchased with a view to resale at a profit. Purchase for any other purpose, such as aesthetic pleasure or capital growth, would not constitute trading. In *Ruthledge* v. *The Commissioners of the Inland Revenue* (1929) it was decided that a person who had bought a million rolls of toilet paper and sold them at a profit was trading since the purchases were unlikely to be either for private use or aesthetic pleasure!

- Badge 2 relates to the period of ownership, a short period of ownership indicating an intention to buy and sell and therefore an indication of trading.
- Badge 3 relates to frequency; where the same types of goods are being purchased and resold frequently this indicates trading.
- Badge 4 relates to processing; where there is some activity to modify or repackage, etc., an object this suggests trading.
- Badge 5 relates to the circumstances of sale; where, for example, an object is sold to provide cash in an emergency this would not indicate trading.
- Badge 6 is the question of profit and motive; an intent to produce a profit suggests trading although the Inland Revenue do point out that a lack of motive to profit will not usually be accepted as an indication that trading was not intended if a profit does arise. The deck is stacked in the Inland Revenue's favour – so what else is new!

With regard to whether or not a person is self-employed, assuming that they are trading or carrying on a professional vocation, there are those who obviously *are* (the man who runs the corner shop, the accountant in practice, the solicitor in practice, and so on), and equally there are those who obviously *are not* (the person employed at the supermarket checkout, the person on the factory production line, the salaried executive in the company's offices). However, between these two extremes is a huge grey area where in practice the Inland Revenue will decide whether or not they will allow you to be self-employed.

[17]

We could term these the badges of the self employment:

- Badge 1 relates to risk. The self-employed man takes financial risks, suffering losses as well as taking profits. Once the job is done the employed man is guaranteed his wage whether or not the customer pays the company he works for. Therefore the question of whether you are taking a risk will determine whether you are genuinely self employed.
- The second badge relates to control and investment; the self-employed person exercises management over how and when to work, who to engage and who to seek advice from. Someone who is not genuinely their own boss is probably not self employed.
- The third badge relates to presentation. When you see a customer do you see them in your own name or in the name of some other company for whom you actually work?
- The fourth badge relates to reward. Payment according to hours worked or specific tasks suggests self employment whereas a regular weekly or monthly (or even hourly) wage irrespective of output suggests working for someone else and therefore an employed position.
- The fifth badge relates to resources and the Inland Revenue consider this one closely. If a person claims to be a painter and decorator then is he using his own equipment or that provided by a main contractor? If the former then he is probably self employed but if the latter then he can hardly be self-employed since if he was not working for

the main contractor he would not be able to work at all, having no equipment of his own.

In addition to these general criteria there are special regulations relating to the building industry and the film industry and the Inland Revenue will no doubt extend these to other industries in the future. Your accountant can advise on these special situations.

When you become self-employed you have a responsibility to inform the Inland Revenue and there is a time limit for making this declaration. Usually your accountant will make the submissions on your behalf but it is of course important that you inform them of your commencement so that the notification can be made within the proper time limit. The time limit is within one year from the end of the first year of assessment. Assessments run from 6th April to 5th April and the first assessment will always run from the date of commencement to the next 5th April; notification must therefore be by the following 5th April. As an example, if your business commenced on 1st August 1990 then the first assessment would run from 1st August 1990 to 5th April 1991 and the notification of commencement must be given to the Inland Revenue by 5th April 1992. Failure to do so will render you liable to penalties and interest.

Your accountant is best advised to make the notification and will have the appropriate documentation to do this; such notification can just take the form of a letter to the Inspector of Taxes but eventually you will be required to complete a form 41G which gives details of you and your business. If you do engage an accountant then you will be required to complete a form 64–8, this being your written authority, on an Inland Revenue letterhead authorising them to discuss your personal taxation affairs with the accountant; they are unable to do so without this form. Your accountant will have these forms and will probably have pre-stamped them with the firm's name.

Briefcase Points

- Full details of the nature of your trade and the way you will be running your business including the working relationship you have with your customer/employer.
- Trading results to date, if any.
- Forecast of the next 12 months' trading results, or details of likely income and expenditure to allow your accountant to build up an estimate.
- Date when you started, or will start; details of your previous employment or self employment including your previous tax reference number.
- Your P45 from your previous employers, or your unemployment benefit office if previously unemployed.
- Your National Insurance number.

TAX ASSESSMENTS

When the Inland Revenue raise a tax bill it is issued in the form of an assessment containing details of income, capital allowances, personal allowances and reliefs, tax rates being charged, National Insurance charges and reliefs, together with other sundry details. You should ensure that your authority form 64–8 is lodged with the Inland Revenue so that your accountant receives a copy of this for checking. I examined two random batches of issues at peak periods in my office and discovered that some 70 per cent of all assessments issued required some form of 'challenge' to the Inland Revenue's figures. Many of these points would not be recognised by the taxpayer, which could result in paying too much tax. One further word of warning: when you receive your copy of the assessment, check that your accountant got one too; even with the 64–8 lodged there are a great many times when the accountant's copy is not issued by the Inland Revenue for one reason or another.

NATIONAL INSURANCE CONTRIBUTIONS FOR THE SELF-EMPLOYED

The self-employed are generally liable to account for Class 2 flat rate National Insurance contributions. They have to make a notification to the Department of Social Security of their commencement of trade so that this can be set up. Payment may be made by stamping a card at the post office or by direct debit from a bank account. There are certain limits, which change annually, below which you can be granted exception from paying these contributions and your accountant will be able to advise you on this and how to make application for exception. In addition, in some businesses such as the performing arts, it is possible to make an application for deferment of Class 2 and Class 4 contributions (see Class 4 below) on the grounds that certain engagements will deduct Class 1 National Insurance (normally employee National Insurance) although recognising your self-employed status for tax purposes. The Department of Social Security calculate the final position at each year-end and notify you of any under- or overpayments made during the year.

In addition to Class 2 you will be liable for Class 4 National Insurance. This is automatically calculated by the Inland Revenue and is based on your profits. Your accountant, however, on receipt of copies of your tax and National Insurance assessments based on your profits, can examine this to ensure that you are being charged the correct amount and that half of the charges have been allowed against tax, which is the current position at the time of writing.

If you are also an employee (in addition to being self employed) then you will be suffering Class 1 National Insurance contributions and your accountant will be able to advise you of the appropriate action to take to avoid overpaying. In these circumstances you must bring with you to the meeting details of your salary from your employment as well as some projection of likely income from your self employment, though your accountant will be able to assist you in preparing the latter.

Briefcase Points

- National Insurance number.
- Details of previous employment or self employment.
- If previously unemployed, details of your benefit office and the P45 issued when you signed off.

THE SELF-EMPLOYED AND VAT

The government sets annually a limit on turnover above which you are required by law to register for VAT

[22]

(Value Added Tax). Your accountant will be aware of this limit and should you exceed it then there are time limits for VAT registration beyond which there are penalties for non-compliance. If you are in any doubt as to whether you should be registered for VAT then you should bring with you all your current information in respect of past and probable future turnover so that your accountant can advise you.

Of more concern is when you may not have reached the VAT limit but may still want to register in any case. Your accountant can advise you whether or not the Customs & Excise are likely to be sympathetic to your application and will inform you of the requirements of voluntary registration, i.e. the way in which you present your business to the Customs & Excise. For them to approve voluntary application they must be satisfied that the self employment is a substantial part of your work and that the work is undertaken with a view to profit on a genuinely commercial basis. They will also need to know either when you are proposing to commence trading or the date from which you believe you need to be or want to be registered.

Your accountant will also be able to advise you if voluntary registration is desirable; it may be that it will enable you to claim back VAT suffered on certain purchases, but if this is minimal then the additional bookkeeping costs may outweigh the advantages. In many cases this is a straight calculation – albeit one which you must weigh up the pros and cons of for yourself – and your accountant can do the figurework necessary to give you the information on which to base your decision.

If you do decide to register for VAT then you will have to account for it, usually on a quarterly basis. There are certain monthly and even annual schemes and your accountant can discuss with you whether they, or your staff will be undertaking the appropriate bookkeeping. Your accountant will also be able to advise you on the pros and cons of joining the cash accounting scheme or the annual accounting scheme. The cash accounting scheme relates to reporting VAT on sales when the money is received rather than when invoices are raised and the annual accounting scheme relates to preparing one annual VAT return having made agreed monthly payments on account to the VAT office. Bringing details of your principal sales and purchases to the meeting will enable the accountant to best advise you on these various options and courses of action.

VAT registration carries with it obligations to maintain certain records adequate for the purpose. Do be aware that when you are VAT registered you become an unpaid tax collector for the government and they have powers to ensure that you are doing their work for them and powers to penalise you if you fail to do so. You may think that it is unfair to be penalised for making mistakes in doing the government's work for them, particularly since you are not paid for it (indeed it will cost you time and possibly money to comply), but if so, then all I can say is you will not be the first to have noticed this! One client who came to me having exceeded the VAT limits listened patiently while I explained his obligations and what the implications were, but obviously I did not make clear his legal position on the first attempt, for having heard what was involved he said to me: 'No, I don't think I will join after all.' It was a great disappointment to him when I explained that whereas Groucho Marx may have been able to decide not to join any club that was prepared to have the likes of him as a member, an invitation from the

VAT Office was to be treated rather like an invitation to dinner from Al Capone: an offer you couldn't refuse!

Briefcase Points

- Think through why you might want to be registered for VAT, even if you don't have to.
- Details of past turnover (sales) and a reasonable estimate of turnover for the next 12 months.

- A description of the nature of your business.
- Details of the products or services that you sell so that your accountant will be able to distinguish between standard-rated, zero-rated and outside-scope items.

WHAT CAN BE CLAIMED FOR

If you are the owner of a business then you have the right to spend business funds on any purpose you deem appropriate. However, only certain items will be allowable for tax purposes and in order to predict your tax liabilities you will need to know which items are allowable and which are not. Your accountant can advise you on this as there is no set definition and the answer will depend on the circumstances of the trade. As an obvious example, a self-employed electrician will have difficulty justifying a claim for the use of a television whereas a TV scriptwriter would find this an essential piece of equipment.

Since self-employed accounts are primarily produced for submission to the Inland Revenue it is important to distinguish between what is and what is not allowable for tax purposes. Further, there will be decisions to be made about how much of home telephone bills, home heat and light and vehicle running relates to the business and how much is private. Wherever there are non-exclusive uses you can discuss with the accountant the basis of your calculation so that this may be presented appropriately to the Inland Revenue. It may be important in the early years to establish a pattern, by keeping accurate mileage records and so on, and your accountant will advise on this. It may be that these claims will be subject to continual review in which case records such as this will have to be kept all the time.

With regard to working from home there are pitfalls in making the wrong claims and opening up a potential capital gains tax liability. The accountant can look at the circumstances of your business and advise on how to plan your tax affairs most expediently. In order to do this he or she must have full information regarding the nature of your business and how these non-exclusive costs are incurred. All of this information should be taken to the meeting with the accountant so that the proper advice may be given.

You will need to distinguish between what are known as 'capital' expenditures and 'revenue' expenditures. Basically, revenue expenditures are deemed to be used up within the year in which they are purchased, whereas capital expenditures are purchased for a longer period of time and have a different treatment for tax purposes. Revenue expenditures are written off against profit in the year in which they are incurred whereas capital expenditures are written off at a statutory rate of, currently, 25 per cent annum on the written down value over a number of years. Your accountant can advise you as to what constitutes capital and what constitutes revenue if you bring with you details of your purchases for the appropriate period.

Before incurring some expenditures it may be wise to discuss their tax treatment with your accountant as there may be advantages to consider between purchase or leasing.

Since there is no practical way to list all the items that are allowable, or all those that are not, given the nature of each individual business, the guideline that must be adhered to here is simply that you should take all of this kind of information to any meeting. This means sufficient information to allow the accountant to understand what is being purchased, what is being sold and the purpose to which each item is being put so that appropriate advice may be given.

Briefcase Point

- Provide your accountant with a concise description, preferably written, of the way you will be running your business, the main equipment and premises you will be using, the products you will sell and the expenses you will have to pay. (Writing it down will clear up a lot of vague points you may be uncertain of yourself!)

KEEPING RECORDS

The exact form of the records you must keep will depend on the business. However, there are certain ground rules.

You must keep records of your income, with as much supporting documentation as possible. If you invoice people for goods or services then keep copies of the invoices. These should be summarised periodically in a Sales Day Book (which can be a book, loose sheets of paper or data stored in a computer system). You will need to know who owes you money and so the records should indicate who has paid you and when they paid. If you have many transactions with each customer then you might consider keeping a Sales Ledger showing the state of your accounts with individuals. Where you do not invoice formally then you will have to keep and summarise other available documentation; till rolls, building site pay-slips, etc.

Similarly, with expenses you should summarise your costs under various headings so that you know what you are spending and you should keep the summaries together with the actual invoices from other people. You will probably not pay all your debts immediately and therefore you must keep records of who you owe money to, and when you paid them. If this is likely to be complex then it is worth formalising this into Purchase Day Books and Purchase Ledgers, similar in principle to their sales equivalents.

If you pay wages then you must keep a record of this in a form that enables you to know who you have paid, what you have paid, what deductions you have made and what has been paid over to the tax offices. There are regulations about the nature of the records you must keep and your accountant can advise on these, in addition to setting up the PAYE system with your appropriate tax office on your behalf.

You should also keep a record of what you have personally drawn out of the business, and of what capital you may have introduced.

If you have stocks then you should keep records of your stock position at any given time. This way you will know what stocks you have and what you need to order, and it will enable you to prepare figures necessary for your year-end balance sheet. Proper stock records will help you to identify those items of stock that do not sell well, or sell exceptionally well, by enabling you to examine the amount of times you turn over the items in the year. Money tied up in stocks is lost to the bank account, and remember the golden rule that *stocks are never sold* – if this seems wrong bear in mind that stocks sold are replaced, and there is always a level on your shelves that, in effect, stays forever. For this reason stock control is one of the most important issues in business planning for many businesses and you should discuss appropriate stock control management from the outset with your accountant who will be able to devise a system that keeps the minimum of cash tied up.

You should keep other records such as your bank statements, your paying-in books and slips, your cheque book stubs and, if possible, your returned cheques.

The actual form of the records you keep can vary considerably; you might buy a simple lined record book, make up your own columns for 'ins' and 'outs' and record your figures in this. In addition you might keep loose summary sheets for Sales Day Books etc. Alternatively you might keep a full set of books in bound form; Cash Book recording the movements in and out of the bank, Petty Cash Book recording cash movements, Sales Day Book Book and Sales Ledgers recording your takings and debtors, Purchase Day Books and Purchase Ledgers recording your expenses and your payments, even a Nominal Ledger and Journal Book.

There is a mid-way alternative available for businesses that are not too complex; books which enable you to record on a weekly basis all the necessary transactions in a specially laid out 'page per week' format. There are similar books available for recording transactions for VAT purposes. There are also a number of 'systems' available for bookkeeping which use carbonised sheets to write up the books and provide summaries of transactions.

Lastly, you might keep your records partly or wholly on computer and there are software packages available, with and without stock control facilities, for most computers.

In addition to the basic books you can keep wages records and VAT records in any of these forms, but special circumstances may dictate a need for special recording; for example if you run a grocer's and take food home from the shop for personal use then these transactions must be recorded even though no money will change hands.

Whatever records you keep you must retain them for at least a six-year period in case they are required for examination; some legal documents, such as leases, long-term contracts and the like, should be kept for longer periods.

Briefcase Points

- Provide your accountant with a concise description, preferably written, of the way you will be running your business, the main equipment and premises you will be using, the products you will sell and the expenses you will have to pay. If you have not designed any books your accountant will be able to assist you to do so.

- If you have already started trading then bring with you whatever records you have already kept (even if it is the not-so-proverbial supermarket carrier bag full of screwed up petrol bills that you found under the sofa that morning!). Based on your existing records your accountant can advise on any improvements that might be necessary (even if it's only to use a carrier bag from a better class of department store!).

WORKING FROM HOME

The question of whether or not you should, or can, work from home involves several considerations. Firstly there is the question of the local authority's attitude to this; depending on the authority – and some are a good deal more restrictive than others – the scope of what you may do will be limited. In practically all cases you will need planning permission. Where you're working alone, employing no staff, and where there are not likely to be visitors to the premises because of your work (which includes customers, suppliers, advisors or deliveries) then you are more likely to get permission. For anything else it is less likely. Certainly the more visitors you are likely to have will make it harder to get permission as the authority will consider the effect of parking on the neighbourhood. Any noise or nuisance your work may create will obviously go against you, and the hours you plan to operate may be important in their decision. Whatever your circumstances you should apply to your local authority who can provide you with a guideline booklet, though they will usually only discuss a complete proposal.

Secondly, there are the tax implications of running a business from home; if you use all of your property for your business, but none of it exclusively, then you will be unlikely to suffer Capital Gains Tax charges on your home when you sell it. (As a private sale of a principal residence it is generally exempt from this.) However, you will only be able to claim allowance in your accounts for what is generally known as 'heat and light', or 'office running'. In other words, because you are working from home the light and heat are on when they would otherwise be off (if you were out, working at an office) and this is regarded as a legitimate expense.

Such costs as rates, water rates, etc. would not be allowed as the Inland Revenue would argue that you would have to pay these whether you worked there or not. If, in fact, you bought a larger property because you needed the space to run your business then claims here might be available but this would re-open the question of a charge to Capital Gains Tax.

Thirdly, you should consider whether there are any other restrictions on your running the business from home; if you are a tenant then there may be prohibitive clauses in your tenancy agreement. There may also be restrictive covenants over the property even if you own it freehold. A solicitor will be able to advise on these matters.

Lastly, you should consider whether you have the appropriate insurances. In every case, however, you should consult the insurance company that deals with your domestic insurances.

Briefcase Points

- Details of the way in which you will be working from home.
- Alternatives you have considered such as an office, office-sharing, using outside secretarial facilities, etc.
- Any lease or other agreements relevant to your property.
- The results of any discussions with your solicitor on this subject. (It may be wise to discuss this with a solicitor before seeing your accountant or you may end up constructing a plan that legally cannot work.)

INSURANCES

All businesses require insurance of some form or another. In some cases it is required by law, in other cases it may well be advisable. In many cases you will have to decide what insurances you can afford, and what insurances you cannot afford to be without! Insurances you will have to consider include:

Public Liability Insurance. If people suffer injury or damage to their property arising out of your business you could have to pay damages. This would be true whether you work from home, in an office or in a factory where, for example, your customers, suppliers or other guests could suffer accidents. It would apply particularly where you were working at someone else's premises as, say, a builder, plumber or electrician would have to do in the nature of his trade. If a plumber blows a hole in the kitchen wall there is bound to be some complaint! Public liability insurance usually covers you up to the expected limits of claims. It can be costly in certain specific trades but that is generally because the risks in those trades are higher and therefore there is all the more reason for insuring against them.

Products Liability Insurance is similar to public liability cover but relates to insuring you against claims that may arise because of injury or damage caused to people or property by the products you sell.

Employer's Liability Insurance is required by law if you have employees. This would be the case even if you only engaged a part-timer or someone for one specific assignment. You are required to hold a certificate proving you have this cover.

Goods In Transit Insurance is specific to certain types of movement of stock, and is designed to protect you from loss should anything happen to your goods whilst being transported.

Domestic Contents Insurance. Generally speaking this covers your personal assets at home against theft or damage. Where you work from home you may have business assets on the premises and these can be covered under this policy. However, it is important that you specify to your insurers the fact that you do work from home and it may be necessary to specify certain assets of high value on the policy. If your policy cannot cover this, then it is advisable to take out a specific *Office Contents Policy.*

Property Insurance is needed to cover damage to your premises and their contents from fire, theft, flood and a host of other eventualities.

All Risks Policy. Where you have specific items of value or where it is necessary for you to take items out of the office it may be necessary to cover these with an all risks policy. Camera equipment which is incidental to your business is one example of this. In the case of specific trades, such as photography, special insurances are usually advised and the relevant trade organisations are generally a good source of information on the best insurances and most reasonable rates available. In addition, you may consider special policies for special circumstances such as damage to computer hardware or software.

Motor Insurance. If the use of your motor car is incidental to your trade then it may well be covered by your normal social, domestic and pleasure policy, but it is as well to check this with the insurance company. Where the car is an essential of the trade then specific cover will probably be needed. As most motor policies do not cover your stocks or assets in the car then some of the policies mentioned earlier may have to be considered.

Life Assurance. It is said that the only certain thing in life is death. As the breadwinner your death can cause hardship to your family and it is advisable to protect them from that by some form of life assurance. This is true whether you are self-employed or in employment. There are a variety of forms of life assurance available from term assurance to endowment policies and it is advisable to consult an insurance broker on what is best for you and your situation.

Health Insurances, sometimes known as *Income Replacement Policies* are designed to provide you with cash if you fall ill or are injured. They are usually subject to a waiting period before you can claim and, as insurances go, are quite expensive. However, the damage to your family's income if you cannot work can be devastating and this can ease the burden on them. There is usually a facility in these policies for compensation if you are severely injured.

Income Protection Policies, also known as *Business Interruption Insurance,* are designed to do what health insurance does, replacing your lost income, but in this case where the loss is due to damage to your premises or equipment rather than your health.

Private Health Insurance. Membership of private medical schemes can be more than a luxury to you as a self-employed person. They give you the ability to choose when and where you are treated for medical conditions, and they can mean a quicker response. In business the saying 'time is money' is very true and time spent waiting to be cured or treated can damage your business – sometimes seriously.

Pensions are a form of insurance. When you are self-employed there will be no company pension plans; what pensions you have you will have to arrange for yourself unless you are planning to live on a state pension when you retire (which will almost certainly mean a considerable drop in your living standards). Pensions, at the time of writing, attract personal tax relief and can therefore help in reducing your overall tax bill. The subject of pensions is a complex topic, examined in a separate chapter.

These are the primary insurances you must consider seriously, and there are others, particularly in certain trades, as we have mentioned. You have to balance the available resources to pay for these insurances against the risk of uninsured loss. You must also bear in mind those policies such as employer's liability insurance which you are required to have by law, or policies which are required by regulations covering your particular industry. In the end you may have to leave some insurances until the business is on a sounder financial footing – it would not be advisable to bankrupt the business just trying to pay an overwhelming list of insurance premiums (mainly because you can't get insurance against so reckless an action!).

Briefcase Points

- Existing insurance and pension policies.
- A written note of your own ideas of the insurances and pensions you think you will need, and why you think you will need them.
- Any advice given by other financial advisers such as insurance brokers.

The 'Briefcase Points' in this chapter are numerous; the accountant for the self-employed is acting as if he or she were the business's internal finance staff. Discussions with your accountant are necessarily complex and involve many areas of the business. Rule one, therefore, is to buy a very big briefcase before getting ready to see your accountant!

3 Limited company audits

Unlike most unincorporated (self-employed) businesses, limited companies are subject to external audit (checking) by qualified accountants. This is a requirement of the Companies Acts. This chapter is therefore specifically about the audit function, though small companies should also read the chapters regarding self employment when considering their accountancy and many other requirements.

An audit is a check on the published accounts of limited companies performed by external qualified accountants who are approved for the purpose. They must remain independent of the company, and must bear in mind that their audit report will be used by many parties who have a need to rely on the accounts of the company.

The audit can last anything from days to months depending on the size of the company, and the work done will involve checking the company's systems (routines) for handling its paperwork as well as testing specific items from documents to ledgers and obtaining external confirmation of figures – checking debtor balances by writing to debtors, creditor balances by writing to creditors, bank details by writing to the bank, and so on.

Perhaps the audit function is also best summed up by looking at the end product – the Audit Report. This forms part of the financial statements (accounts) and is intended to be read as a part of those statements. A 'clean' audit report, in other words one that does not report on problems within the company, would read something like this:

> We have audited the financial statements on pages — to —. Our audit was conducted in accordance with approved Auditing Standards. In our opinion the financial statements, which have been prepared under the historical cost convention, give a true and fair view of the state of the Company's affairs at (year-end date) and of its result and source and application of funds for the year then ended and comply with the Companies Act 19—

A brief explanation of some of these terms is appropriate;

- 'approved Auditing Standards'. These are determined by the approved auditing bodies such as the Institute of Chartered Accountants or the Association of Certified Accountants. They are not law in the strict sense, but have the same force from the auditor's point of view since they are subject to scrutiny by their regulatory bodies.
- 'the historical cost convention'. A standard basis of reporting costs, etc., details of which are not essential for this book. Breaches of that convention have to be reported.
- 'true and fair view'. This is very important; the accounts are *not* expected to be 100 per cent accurate; allowance is given in both the bookkeeping and the audit for errors if they are not material, in other words if they do not affect an

overall appreciation of the figures in the accounts. (One student in an auditing exam is reported to have answered a question about audit reports stating that 'the accounts must show a fairly true view'. He is probably making a good living as an estate agent by now!)

- 'comply with the Companies Act'. This is the law regulating companies and breaches have to be reported.

In the case of smaller companies there is a paragraph which may be inserted into the audit report which amounts to virtually no qualification whatsoever, and results from the fact that some companies are 'owner-run'. This paragraph would read something like:

In common with many businesses of similar size and organisation the Company's system of control is dependent upon the close involvement of the directors, who are also the shareholders. Where independent confirmation of the completeness of the accounting records was not available we have accepted assurances from the directors that all the Company's transactions have been reflected in the accounts.

Having looked at the end product of an audit we can consider who benefits from it. The report is directed to the owners, usually the shareholders, of the company. It tells them whether or not the directors have been running the company properly on their behalf and in their best interests, and whether appropriate laws and regulations have been complied with. It must be remembered that the shareholders are not allowed access to the day-to-day running and management details of their company. This may seem absurd at first but it is in fact logical – it prevents a competitor from acquiring all your management information simply by buying one share in your company.

For small companies the position becomes slightly absurd; if the directors are also the shareholders (in a 'husband-and-wife' company for example) then the audit amounts to telling Mr and Mrs Smith that Mr and Mrs Smith have been acting properly and in Mr and Mrs Smith's own best interests. For this reason there have been suggestions that the audit requirement should be removed for such companies. Such a move might however be resisted by other groups such as creditors, banks and loan companies, who rely on the audit as a confirmation that the company is being properly managed. The audit can be seen, therefore, to have wider implications than merely its stated purpose.

With regard to your company's appointment of auditors, it is usual to appoint the same firm to be both accountants and auditors. The auditors can come only from a limited number of sources. Approved auditing Members of the Institute of Chartered Accountants, and of the Association of Certified Accountants are the two main ones. In addition there are a few individuals especially approved by the Department of Trade.

You should confirm that the auditors you appoint are legally able to take on the job; I once exposed an individual who had been signing audit reports for years and was not qualified or approved – luckily no harm had resulted though the company might have been held liable if an outside party relying on the audit report had suffered loss.

Many of the selection criteria for those that are therefore available are the same as for choosing your accountant (see Chapter 1). One minor point to bear in mind however is that, unlike accountants who can be dismissed without ceremony (see Chapter 17), auditors have certain rights of office granted to them by the Companies Acts. This is because they are in the curious position of being appointed by the directors to report to the shareholders on the activities of the directors. If the directors dismiss them it could be because the auditors have uncovered something the directors would rather the shareholders did not know. For this reason the Companies Acts provide for the auditors to have a right of statement to the shareholders.

Look for people with experience in your field of work; it will stop them having to ask obvious and silly questions it they are conversant with your industry's specific areas. That said, the majority of audit work is the same in principle whatever type of company is being studied, so this is not an absolute requirement. But there are other considerations. One would be the advantage of a recommendation with regard to standards of work, working practices and so on; you need to feel you can work with your auditors. On this point, consider finding a firm that does more than just look at the books and go away; the audit firm should back up the audit with recommendations and advice so that you are getting the best from the time these specialists are spending with your records.

Audit firms vary in size from individuals working from home to huge multi-national businesses with offices all across the world. You should choose a firm appropriate to the size of your business. However, this does not have to be the size of the business as it is, but rather the size of the firm as you reasonably expect it to be in the near future – give yourself room to grow. If you do not need international or national connections don't pay for them; for many smaller businesses the smaller end of the market is quite appropriate. The larger firms are there to serve the larger companies.

Fees for audit work are higher than general accounts preparation because of the levels of work, responsibility and legal exposure; but they can be quoted at the initial meeting just as easily as accountancy costs. Meetings with your auditors will vary according to circumstances. The audit can take place either at your premises or theirs, depending on the requirements of the audit and the management and organisation of the business. If at your premises, then the records will of course be there; if at the auditor's then you must arrange to take all the year's records with you.

There are certain legal requirements regarding records that must be fulfilled. With small, unincorporated businesses it is not unusual for the accountant to find clients bringing the year's receipts in a carrier bag and dropping them on the desk; this may not be the best way to run a business throughout the year, but it breaches no law. However, to comply with the Companies Acts the books and records of the company must be maintained throughout the year – a condition of a 'clean' audit report.

The more work you do, the less the accountant or auditor has to do and the less fees will have to be charged. If you present maintained ledgers to the accountants who then have to prepare the accounts this will be charged for; if your own bookkeeping allows for a set of accounts to be prepared and delivered to the auditors then those fees are saved. It is highly advisable therefore to do as much of the accountancy as you can before handing over the records; it will also identify errors or omissions and eliminate the auditors' need to raise queries, extend checking and so on as they can rely better on your own work.

That said, you must remember that there are audit functions you *cannot* do, and which must be done by the auditor in order to provide an independent review of the accounts. You cannot arrange the debtors' or creditors' enquiries (called 'circularisations'), though you can assist in the mechanics once the auditor has selected the sample. You cannot get the bank's confirmation for the auditor who must apply for this and receive your bank's reply personally. You cannot select which documents the auditor will or will not examine; it must be the auditor's choice. And obviously, you cannot do any basic audit work on behalf of the auditors; it would defeat the purpose.

The main points in being ready for the audit, therefore, are to be as up to date with the records as possible, to have eliminated as many questions, errors or omissions as possible, and to have available with easy access the books, records, source invoices, bank statements and so on that the auditor will need. It is a good idea to write to the auditors ahead of the annual audit and make the arrangements that suit both their office and your own staffing and organisational arrangements. Make sure that any key staff that the auditor will need to speak to are not on holiday; make sure *you* are not on holiday. Do not pick busy times in your business cycle for the audit, pick a date when you can spare the necessary time and effort for the auditors (firework retailers should *not* pick the last week in October first week in November for the audit, for example!).

In your letter to the auditors confirm what books and records they will want to see, particularly in the first days of the audit, and have them ready. Too often I have arranged audits and spent the first day wandering around behind the client while he tries to find the books that should have been ready – and I usually make the effort to contact the client to make sure they know what requirements I have as well as checking on their own.

Perhaps it is an obvious perspective for someone in my position to take but I would also suggest that you view your work with the auditors as a partnership designed principally for your benefit. The auditor is there to help, not hinder. Certainly you are being 'checked up on', but if there are problems to be identified then for the most part their elimination is to your benefit. If ways to improve your 'systems' (the way you do things) can be suggested then that is also to your benefit. If, of course, you are a director who is stealing from the till, putting through your horse-betting debts as 'charitable donations to sick animals', having your house swimming-pool installed as a 'fire-prevention reservoir' or the like, then by all means view the auditors with hostility – burglars probably view the police in a similar way. For the most part the perception of auditors as a necessary evil is the result of failing to take advantage of a valuable company adviser.

To show just how concerned some companies are about audit visits to their premises I reproduce below a memo that was distributed in one company, which was passed to me by an amused, sympathetic (and, perhaps significantly, ex-) secretary.

MEMORANDUM TO ALL STAFF
CONFIDENTIAL

On (date) and for a period of approximately (x) weeks the auditors from (audit company name) will be on site. The following guidelines are to be followed in any meeting or proposed meeting with the members of the audit staff.
1. Answer questions raised in short, simple language. If you elaborate or waffle the auditor may accidentally learn something he is not entitled to.
2. Never allow yourself to be engaged in 'casual' conversation; auditors are never 'off-duty' and they will use against you anything they can pick up at any time.
3. Never answer a question that relates to someone else, or to another site or department. If such a question is asked of you, that question must be reported to your supervisor or manager as soon as possible.

4. Never guess an answer. If you need to look up information then ask for time to do so. You cannot be expected to hold all information in your head at all times, but if you give a wrong answer the auditors will hold it against you.

5. If the auditors indicate errors in your work or the work of your section then you may verbally acknowledge the point and inform them that you will discuss the matter with your supervisor or manager. *Never* sign an acknowledgement of error should one be offered unless this has been agreed upon with your supervisor or manager.

6. Auditors on visits to (a number of locations were listed) must be accompanied at all times. It is acceptable for auditors to talk to (a list of staff gradings was given) but note all questions and answers given and report these to your manager or supervisor at the earliest opportunity.

7. Be polite. Auditors are often rude and 'offish' but if there [sic] manner causes you anger you may say something in the heat of the moment that should not be said.

8. Never make critical comments of other people, personnel or departments.
END MEMO

There would be times when such an attitude might be explainable, such as during a 'hostile' takeover bid, but this was not the case here, and in any case this is not the only example I have seen or heard of. It would be easy to dismiss such a memo as being from 'someone with something to hide' but I really feel it comes from a deeper-seated fear that is quite irrational and certainly unfortunate. I would not recommend the memo as a list of preparations for an audit. Rather, I would suggest the directors (if they haven't got swimming-pool fire-reservoirs of course!) sit down with the auditors and discuss what benefits both can obtain from this partnership. Audit fees are high; spend them sensibly.

It is worth noting that there are other organisations that need an audit, though under different legislations; solicitors and charities for example. The commonsense rules in respect of selecting, and working with, your auditors still apply of course.

Briefcase Points

- Ensure that your auditors are legally able to do the audit – check with their governing body or the Department of Trade.
- Plan the audit with your auditors ahead of time.
- Ensure the right staff are available.
- Ensure *you* are available.
- Ensure that your books and records are as up to date and reconciled (balanced and checked) as possible.
- Ensure that the books and all other documents relating to the year being audited are available, arranged in logical order and are easy to use.
- Cover up the house 'fire-prevention reservoir' with a large tarpaulin and claim it is 'something to do with the drains'. (Only joking!)

---

4   Restructuring your business

As is the case in most sections of this book, preparation for a meeting with an accountant with a view to restructuring your business is going to depend on the specific circumstances. You may be seeking a change to replace a first generation of directors with their sons and daughters, it may be that the company is enjoying incredible growth and success, or suffering near disaster.

However, as usual, there is some basic material that probably applies to almost all situations. This is the material for the first meeting since neither you nor the accountants will yet have a full grasp of the 'big picture'. Many of the details needed will be similar to those required for management consultancy (see Chapter 8), and in preparing for this meeting that chapter should also be studied. In addition to that material you should also:

- prepare a financial history of the company for the past five years, or since commencement if less. Restructuring often depends on trends, and trends take time to emerge so a 'history lesson' is in order. The trends will give the accountants a good idea not just of where you are presently, but how you got there;

- have ready your proposals. What exactly do *you* want from this rearrangement? You must accept from the outset that your accountant may debate with you the wisdom of your choice, but that debate is fruitless if you have no strong idea of your own requirements;

- have ready your *reasons* for change as you see them. Again, these may be subject to debate but if you have cleared your own thinking then the discussion will have direction. In an extreme case I dealt with, the reasons presented to me were the company's recent successes; in fact a detailed analysis showed the problem to be addressed was an underlying deterioration that promised to bankrupt the company;

- have ready your plan of *how* you propose to make the changes. It would be surprising if your accountant – with a wider view and possibly more experience – did not have alternative suggestions to offer but clearly the views of the directors are necessary for complete understanding. If the suggestions are sound, then the fact that at least the Board are committed to them will make implementation that much easier;

- bring with you a written list of your other advisers; solicitors, consultants (if not part of your accountant's firm), your bankers, pensions advisers and so on. It would not hurt to jot down some notes of your opinions of the value to your business of these other advisers; the accountants will need to know who to rely on, who is supportive of the company and who seems to have lost faith in its future or interest in its present;

- be sure to bring with you any reports that management consultants (other than from within the accountants own firm) have presented to you. Clearly there will be some overlap, and you do not want to end up paying for the same work twice.

The accountant will need to have some idea of your thinking in order to find a solution that suits your needs. This is something that will arise from discussion, but the clearer your own position then the more fruitful the debate.

As can be seen from the above, the Big Message in preparing for this meeting is to take time to think out your own position ready for discussion. If you walk into your accountant's office and start by saying 'I think my company could do with some sort of change but I haven't given much thought to what,' don't be surprised if it takes a good few meetings – and not a few visits to your chequebook – before you seem to get anywhere. (And it is surprising just how many people start meetings that way.)

If change is being forced on the company from outside then bring whatever material, correspondence and so on, is available from that outside party. This may be the bank, creditors (or a particular creditor), other loan institutions, the shareholders, etc. Clearly, outside parties will be suggesting change for their good, not yours, but your own advisers will look for ways to deal with the problems (and therefore address the issues raised by the outside parties) in a way that is primarily for *your* good.

Above all, recognise that your advisers are there for your benefit alone; once you have decided to place trust in them, do so and never hold back information that could have a bearing on their decisions. However confidential a point may seem to you, it will be (had certainly better be!) respected as confidential by the accountants. They cannot work in the dark, or even in only partial light.

GOING PUBLIC

One particular type of restructuring is known generally as 'going public'. This means that the company enters the stock market. The full procedures are beyond the scope of this book, and the accountant is only one of many advisers that are needed. Furthermore, it is not usually a question of you preparing for this meeting; it is often a case of the accountant suggesting going public as a result of the meetings described above and from that point on the accountant will advise accordingly. A few general points may be of use however:

- the reasons for going public are to raise money for the company and the existing shareholders, to establish a value for the company, to lose close company status for tax purposes and often to assist in a management buy-out;
- the ways of going public are by *placing*, where shares are offered by a sponsor mostly to its own clients, *offer for sale* where the shares are offered to the public by advertisement, and *introduction* where no additional capital is sought and where there are already sufficient shareholders to satisfy requirements.

[53]

Advantages of going public

a) money is raised without incurring fixed repayment and interest commitments
b) finance raised is permanent and not repayable
c) existing shareholders are able to unlock their capital
d) share issues can be used as part of an acquisition or merger.
e) a company's credit and general status is usually improved by entry to the stock market.

Disadvantages of going public

a) the company becomes subject to increased disclosure requirements
b) shareholders will exert pressure for improved dividends
c) the company becomes a potential target for take-overs
d) costs of going public can be high and development finance may be needed.

Briefcase Points

- A five-year history of the business, or a history from the start if more recent.
- Your written ideas of what changes you want to see, why you want them and how you think they should be brought about. (The purpose of writing them down is to focus your mind on matters you might be unconsciously ignoring!)
- A list of your other principal advisers.
- Any reports or recommendations from other advisers.
- Any correspondence relating to outside parties who might be forcing change on you.

---

5 Buying another business

A very important reason for seeing an accountant arises when someone proposes buying out an existing business. This can be an advantage over starting from scratch on your own but needless to say carries some risks with it, many of which arise from the question 'Why is the business being sold in the first place?' When you are buying a business you are actually buying several different components, all of which require a good deal of thought and all of which your accountant is able to advise on.

A worthwhile job of investigation in this regard can be quite costly and the accountant will have to spend a good deal of qualified time in examining the records that you will be presenting. These will include the past accounts of the company, any management accounts and projected accounts, details of the company's advertising and products, any leaflets the company issues and so on. It will be money well spent, however, even if at the end of the day you are writing out a cheque to the accountant who advised you not to buy the company. Remember that a company being sold will be made to look as good as possible and that only when you have bought it, and you are operating it, will you see the truth for what it really is.

And even if you manage to peel off the rind, a lemon is still a lemon. Take the advice of someone who eats fruit for a living!

WHAT ARE YOU GETTING FOR YOUR MONEY?

Fixed Assets

Part of what you will be paying for relates to equipment and long-term assets to be used in the long-term maintenance of the business. This will include premises either on freehold or long leasehold in some cases. Freehold premises may be shown in the accounts at a particular valuation and it is likely that such premises will have been valued as part of the sale price. The question of whether the valuation is truly independent arises and the accountant may be able to advise on ways in which an independent valuation can be had. This will possibly result in a lower agreed price if the initial valuation was rather 'optimistic'. The premises will carry with them obligations for rates, maintenance and other costs and the accountant can advise on these partly from the proposed contracts and partly from the existing accounts.

With regard to equipment, cars, and so on, there will be the question of their useful life and whether they will soon need replacement. If so, has the company, or the would-be owner of the company, got the sums to replace them? – Otherwise he will be out of business very shortly, unable to manufacture the goods necessary to keep going. You should have physically examined these assets to ensure that they are in the sort of working condition you would expect, given the price you are being asked to pay for them.

Stock

Stock is an asset and so it would seem that the more there is the better off you are. This would certainly be true if we were talking about pound notes in the bank, but in the case of stock it is not.

A large quantity of stock can reveal several problems. Firstly, stock control may not have been very successful and the business may have a good deal of its working capital tied up in stock that is sitting on the shelves when the money should be earning interest in the bank. Secondly, the existence of high stocks may mean that the company's products are no longer in demand and that could well be the reason why the proprietor wishes to sell the business in the first place. Thirdly, there is the question of title to stock and it is possible that the proprietor selling the business has overstocked to make the balance sheet look good but in fact not properly reflected the liability for the stocks (in effect claiming title to goods he actually does not own). While this would not be allowed in an audited set of accounts it may well 'slip by' into a management set of accounts prepared for the purpose of the sale of the business.

Work in Progress

There will be a certain amount of goods in the process of creation or a certain number of unfulfilled orders which the company is processing for its customers. The accountant will be able to advise on the valuation which the accounts show for such work in progress or open orders. This is often an area where sellers become rather optimistic as to the value of their own customers' promises.

Goodwill

In many cases the seller will expect the buyer to pay for goodwill and this is a perfectly normal demand. However, it could well be that the goodwill is overstated and indeed many companies that are being sold are often in that state because they have in effect generated badwill, i.e. customers are giving up the company because of poor service, poor quality products and so on. The accountant will be able to advise on the

basis of goodwill valuation and whether or not it is realistic in the circumstances. Goodwill is usually based on a combination of asset value generating income and the generated profits over past years.

It is worthy of note, by the way, that goodwill purchased should be written off over (usually) three years as it is deemed that by the time you have been running the business for that period of time any good-will then existing is that which you have generated and not the goodwill you purchased.

The accountant will also be able to advise on miscella-neous items such as whether you will need to buy or license copyrights, trademarks, etc. and, in conjunction with the solicitors, will be able to advise on protective covenants that should be in the sale contract. In particu-lar, the selling proprietor should not be able to 'open-up shop' nearby in competition with you and thereby steal back all the customers you have effectively bought.

The accountant will examine the business accounts and discuss their significance with you. This is dis-cussed in detail below but a general point is worth making here: the last set of accounts prior to the sale may well show a significant increase in turnover or profit. This – the proprietor may well tell you – is because the business is now booming, making it an absolutely plum choice for you to part with your money for. On the other hand what he will not discuss with you is the probability that in order to pump up the turnover and profits he has put through every sale he can lay his hands on (including selling his grandmother quite probably), some of which he may have been concealing from the Inland Revenue in former years. In other words the business is not growing; indeed it may be shrinking. There are some analyses the accountant can assist you with which are discussed shortly which will suggest whether or not this is true.

As an alternative, the proprietor may say to you 'under the table': 'Actually the figures are really very much better than this but I always keep a bit in my back pocket and away from the Inland Revenue'. Don't believe a word of it! He may well make a habit of doing just that but in the last year prior to the sale – and particularly in any management set of accounts – he would have put through everything he could in order to make the business look as good as possible. The management accounts you are looking at almost certainly reflect the best, if not better than, achievable results.

Another simple point is worthy of consideration: anyone prepared to steal from the Inland Revenue is presumably quite happy to steal from you.

UNDERSTANDING THE ACCOUNTS

There are a number of basic tests and ratios which the accountant can perform on the supplied accounts for a series of years which will indicate the financial soundness of the company and reveal the underlying trends in the business. Firstly, there is what is known as the *current ratio*. This is the ratio of current assets to current liabilities, i.e. the extent to which the liabilities the business has to meet within one year can be met by the existing assets such as stocks, work in progress, debtors, cash at bank and in hand, and so on. Because liabilities can be called in immediately but some assets require time to realise, e.g. stock needs to be sold, work in progress possibly needs to be completed before it is in a position for sale and debtors need to be chased, then a ratio of something like 2:1 is regarded as reasonable. If the current ratio falls significantly lower, say to 1:1 or below, then the company may be either heading for insolvency (or already be there).

There is a second test called the *'acid test'* which also compares current assets to current liabilities but where 'current assets' excludes stocks or any other difficult-to-realise items. The idea of this is that the more immediate assets which can be realised are available to pay the liabilities should they be demanded. It is held that something around 1:1 is acceptable; very much lower may again indicate potential insolvency. (A very high figure may suggest that the company is holding far too much cash and that may reflect bad management on the company's part – not using its assets effectively. Such a consideration would have to be thought through with regard to other management positions.)

The ratio of *creditors to purchases* should be examined, which will indicate the average debt owed by the company. The figure arrived at is actually meaningless as it will reflect many circumstances relating to that particular industry, or that particular point in time, but this is one ratio in particular which should be examined over a time series, i.e. looking at the last five sets of accounts to see whether the position is improving or deteriorating. A deteriorating position indicates that the company is strapped for cash and is having increasing difficulties in paying its creditors. This may represent an underlying problem.

There is a similar figure for debt collection which is the measure of success that the company is having in collecting its credit sales. A deteriorating figure of debt collection, or debt outstanding, will indicate that the company is either being poorly managed or is so desperate that it is making reckless sales and suffering increasing potential bad debts, many of which will be debtors you are being asked to pay for but whose money will never actually materialise.

There are other tests such as *gross profit ratio* and *net profit ratio,* i.e. the percentage profit made on sales before and after overheads. Again, these ratios mean very little unless examined over time but a deteriorating gross or net profit ratio indicates that the company is perhaps unable to increase its prices in the same way that its costs are going up. This may indicate that the company's products are not so popular, either because of quality or some market changes, and it is this deterioration which may have inspired the proprietor to get out while the going is still good enough.

Another analysis is an examination of the profit coming back to the owner, i.e. available to him personally, as a proportion of the total investment he has in the business. In many cases, particularly during recessions, it would be true to say that for all the effort business proprietors put in throughout the year they would, at least on paper, be better off selling their companies and putting the money in the building society where they would earn a greater profit! This is of course overly simplistic but certainly a time series analysis of the return on capital invested in the business will reveal something about the proprietor's motives for selling and something about the likely return that you are going to get on the significant investment that you will have to make to purchase the business.

It may also be that you will have to borrow money, and therefore pay interest, in order to raise the capital to buy the business. In this event that cost of borrowing will be an additional charge which can easily turn a marginal net profit into a marginal net loss and no company will survive long while it is continually making losses.

The accountant will not only be able to examine the accounts in time series for the same company but also will have some idea of the likely results expected from similar companies in the same field. The published accounts of limited companies can be obtained from Companies House and some comparisons made in this way. There are also services which provide anonymous sets of accounts in detail for comparison purposes, which the accountant can utilise in order to advise on the company in relation to its competitors.

Whatever reason the outgoing proprietor has for selling, it is almost certain that they have in some way lost interest in the company and there may well be scope for improvement. However, it is very often the case that the would-be buyer is overly enthusiastic about what he or she would be able to achieve and the accountant can help by removing the rose-tinted glasses and pointing out what can realistically be achieved over a given period of time. It is all very well to believe that certain changes are possible but if they are going to take ten years and the bank will be clamouring for the return of its investment in five then someone has to make this clear to the would-be buyer.

At the end of the day the price paid for a business is very much a matter of bargaining and for all the sophistication that goes into the arguments on either side the only price ever paid for any company is a balance between what the proprietor wants and what the buyer is prepared to pay. This can never be more than an intuitive judgement in the final analysis, but there are, as we have seen, many analyses which can be made leading up to that final judgement which the accountant is best placed to advise upon.

Briefcase Points

- Information on how you came to know the company was up for sale.
- Accounts for the past three to five years.
- Management accounts.
- Projected accounts of likely future trading.
- Any publicity or leaflets issued by the company in the course of its trading.
- Proposed contract of sale, price being asked and terms of settlement being requested.
- Specific details of premises owned or used by the company together with leases, title deeds, details of rents, rates, etc.
- Details of equipment owned, leased or rented by the company.
- Details of stocks or work in progress at the current time, the proposed date of sale, and as much historical data as possible.
- Details of the company's key personnel. In the case of directors, details of existing service contracts.
- Details of any compensations for loss of office that may result from the buy-out.
- Details of the company's sub-contractors.
- Details of the company's main suppliers and customers.
- Any correspondence or other material that has been supplied to you by either the company or its advisers.
- Any opinions or recommendations made by your other advisers, such as solicitors.
- Details of your other advisers, whether or not you have yet consulted them.
- Your own CV giving details of why you think you have the necessary experience or background to run the company.

6   Being bought out

It may be that you are approached by an individual or a company who wishes to buy your business from you. Before making any decision you should consult with your accountant about any offer made. It may be that the enquiry is tentative, with no real offer, but even so a preliminary discussion with your accountant can clear your mind on many points that are going to arise.

The first question is going to be: are you happy with the idea of selling out or are you opposed to the idea? In the case of 'one-man bands' or small family companies the problem is easily resolved; if you don't want to sell at any price then you can decide not to and that is effectively that. However, in the case of larger businesses the directors (who may hold no, or only a minority of, shares) may be put under pressure from some shareholders to accept the offer. In that case the directors must take advice so that they can first decide whether they are right to be hostile to the offer, and if so, how best to resist it and – not unimportantly – explain that decision to the shareholders. Clearly there is some conflict of interest here in that the potential new board of directors may well have ideas about changing the existing board, who are therefore in the position of safeguarding their own necks, possibly over and above the interests of the company.

In order to assess any offer made you should take with you to your accountants (and possibly other advisers):

- Details of any price offered, including any break-down of the components of that price given by the offering company. If no price has been suggested then there will possibly be some preliminary correspondence that indicates the price range being considered.
- The terms affecting the existing directors or owners. It may be that the offer specifically grants the directors a service contract for a period of years, or alternatively makes clear that the existing board will be made redundant in which case the terms of their 'pay-off' will be of interest. In the case of some companies, usually smaller ones though not exclusively so, there may be a requirement for key personnel – and often the self-employed person who is selling the business – to continue working for the company for a specific period while the new owners 'get their feet under the table'. These terms will be of interest to the accountants partly because they can become bargaining factors in agreeing the eventual price.
- Any specific conditions imposed on whether, where or when the selling owners can 'open-up shop' again. In the case of directors it is unlikely that any contract could be enforced that would prevent them taking a job with the company's competitors, but certainly for self-employed or small family-owned companies there is often a requirement that an agreement be signed not tc

compete for customers or clients in the same location for a specific period of time. This makes good sense as part of the sale price will include goodwill, i.e. the perceived value of the company's loyal customers. The buyer does not want all the customers he has 'bought' running off to the old owners under a new name.

- The terms of payment which are, of course, also crucial. Agreeing a price is meaningless if the seller does not get the money. The accountants can advise on the pitfalls of payment structures; they will examine offers of staggered payments and calculate the additional cost to you of lost interest on the money being deferred, and they will advise on guarantees to be sought to protect you against non-payment. They may well advise standing firm and insisting that all the money be available on exchange of contracts; that the buyer's bank should finance the deal and not you.

In the case of one small company I dealt with, an offer was made for buy-out of the existing owners at a price based on future turnover. In essence there would have been a small payment made on transfer, with remaining sums to be paid over the next three years depending on the profits of those later years. There was perhaps a certain reasoning behind the offer – that the company seemed to promise good profits but might not, and the proprietor was of a mind to accept the offer, feeling sympathy for this point of view.

I disagreed most strongly. Audited accounts were available, and we could support those with up-to-date management figures with external documentary evidence such as invoices, bank statements and so on. I felt that if there was a risk to be taken it should be borne by the buyer, not the seller, as is the case for anyone setting out in business; *caveat emptor*, and all that! Further, the price the owners would receive would be dependant on the success of the new owners and not based on the efforts of the current owners over the past years. Apart from being inequitable, this was dangerous; firstly because if the new owners turned out to be incapable then the outgoing owners would be the ones to suffer, and secondly (with all due respect to my colleagues and to Companies Acts legislation), 'creating' a reduced profit in the first few years would not be difficult, thereby possibly keeping back funds from the sellers. To agree the exact formula for profit is not impossible, but it usually leaves open a mass of loopholes for enforcement which may end up with buyer and seller locked in court arguments for years to come. My client took my advice on this one and resisted the offer. We secured a much more stable deal that allowed him to retire with security.

If selling a business it is worth remembering that there are two sides of the fence: the buyer's and the seller's. Therefore you should also read Chapter 5 of this book, 'Buying another business'. Many of the criteria there are relevant to the negotiations and it is wise, as the seller, to know what it is like to stand in the buyer's shoes in order to understand fully the complexity of the debates.

Briefcase Points

- Your briefcase should have the same information in it as for 'Buying another business' (page 64).

---

7 Franchising

Starting a business of your own means creating the vehicle in which you will be trading (i.e. a sole trader or partnership, limited company or one of several less common types of business entity), doing the market research and advertising, finding suppliers and maintaining the market. In franchising these are mostly dealt with by the franchisor (i.e. the person issuing the franchise), leaving the franchisee running a proven business. Examples of successful franchises include Wimpy and McDonald's fast food outlets, Tie Rack, The Body Shop, Snap-On Tools, Home Tune, and many others.

Franchising is a hybrid, lying somewhere between employment and self employment. The franchisor sets up a brand name, often initially by running a successful business, and the franchisees operate within strict guidelines to ensure that all outlets are to the same standard and design.

Although as a franchisee you might believe you are about to be your own boss, in practice this is not the case. As a franchisee you will have a very restrictive contract and you must keep to it because retail premises or business outlets all have to be maintained to an identical standard. The vast majority, if not all, of the goods sold must come from the franchisor and the franchisor has the right to withdraw the franchise if the contract is not maintained. In some ways you, as franchisee, have the best of both worlds; self employment within a huge corporate structure and a national, or international, brand name. However, you also have the worst of both worlds; not really being your own boss since the franchisors have considerable power over what you may or may not do and lacking the protection that would be given to employees through the various employee legislations.

Anyone considering taking up a franchise should consult an accountant, along with other business advisers such as a solicitor. The accountant will be able to analyse the proposed franchise agreement and may be able to identify particularly good or bad contracts.

In particular, the accountant will advise on the presence of certain areas in the franchise contract. For example, the franchisor should be responsible for some support, technical expertise and training, and there should be group advertising (to which the franchisee will contribute on some basis, usually a percentage of turnover). The area in which your franchise operates should be exclusive to you. There are greedy franchisors who issue too many franchise agreements in an area, thereby diluting the earning potential of each franchisee.

There are many pitfalls the accountant will be familiar with: creatively presented accounting data, heavy 'up-front' investment requirements, excessively high royalty fees, inappropriately stated advertising schemes and pyramid selling (which amounts to the franchisee having the right simply to sell more franchises down the chain; aside from the dubious legality of such schemes, usually nobody benefits except those at the top of the pyramid).

When meeting with an accountant to discuss whether to take up a franchise it is obviously essential that the accountant be briefed with the franchisor's name in order to obtain necessary information ahead of the meeting. You should take with you anything from the franchisors, particularly their publicity handouts, copies of draft contracts, some examples of their advertising and details of their profit projections. The accountant will wish to analyse the claims in some detail and, where possible, compare results to projections previously made.

Most of the large well-known franchises will act appropriately but even then there can be difficulties which might affect the individual franchisee; the accountant can discuss these with you in detail. For the lesser-known franchises, or those just entering the market, presumably the brainchild of an entrepreneur bringing a new scheme to bear, there will be a tendency for more projection than track record. The accountant will identify what is hype and what is contractual and will be able to differentiate between reasonable expectation and wild and unreasonable promise. In the United States, where franchising is much bigger business than in the UK, there is specific legislation to protect franchisees. No such legislation exists in the United Kingdom, therefore much prior research and professional advice from accountants and, equally importantly, solicitors, is vital.

Once you have decided to take up the franchise the accountant can also advise on ways of raising the necessary capital to start; remember though that are many successful franchise arrangements but few 'get-rich quick' schemes. For the majority it is a comfortable

way of earning a reasonable living, though often with long hours. However, there are a good number of blood-curdling franchising stories that got away from the Hammer horror movies and your accountant can assist in avoiding the worst – or at least letting you walk into the situation with your eyes wide open from awareness rather than shock!

Briefcase Points

- Franchise name and details of known existing outlets. In the case of 'established' franchises they will supply a full pack of information about the business. Take this to the accountant.
- Any handout publicity, generated by the franchisor. (What are they saying about themselves?)
- Any press or other media material *not* generated by the franchisor. (What are others saying about them?)
- Any proposed contract.
- Where you are buying an existing outlet, details of the past three to five years' accounts for that business.
- Where you are proposing to start a new outlet, details of the income and purchases of the past three to five years of a similar-sized unit to the one you propose.
- Projections made either by the existing franchisee, or by the franchisor.
- Read Chapter 5, 'Buying another business', and include details from the briefcase points given on page 64.

8 Seeking management consultancy

There are specific firms of management consultants, quite different from accountancy firms. However, some accountancy firms do have consultancy arms, and some smaller accountancy practices undertake consultancy, or work with other consultants. To the extent that your accountants can provide such services there are obvious advantages in that they already know your business. At the very least, your accountant ought to be able to suggest the right consultants for the job. For the purpose of this section I will refer to 'consultant' as I have elsewhere in this book referred to 'accountant', but they could well be the same person or firm.

The difficulty in advising how to prepare for a meeting with a consultant, or how to get the best out of one, when needing management consultancy services, is that most clients have very little idea of what they really need. Those that do are usually surprised to find that what are eventually identified as their needs are not what they expected. However, management consultancy usually results in identifying some desirable or necessary changes in a business and before that can be done the existing company must be fully understood by the adviser. The advice applies to all sizes of companies though some points (such as details of the company yacht!) might be more appropriate to larger companies.

In preparing for the meeting you should collate the following information and bring it with you:

- Geographical location of company premises, including any retail outlets, office premises, manufacturing areas and so on. The consultants will need this both to analyse where the company is at present and to investigate areas of major cost saving. Premises can be sold off to release funds (if they are found to be surplus), they can be sold-and-leased-back (effectively exchanging a long-term commitment (the lease) for instant cash (the sale) which may solve an immediate problem), or alternative uses can be found for the premises, some of which you may not have considered.
- A company organisation chart, such as the simplified example shown. This shows the key poeple working in the company and may indicate areas

EXAMPLE OF ORGANISATION CHART

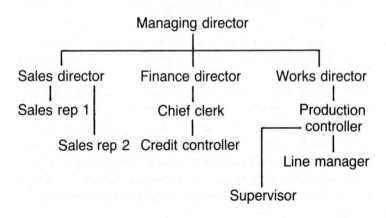

[75]

of deficiency. Along with the chart you should provide CVs (descriptions) of the key personnel; their experience with the company (and prior to joining it), their perceived strengths and weaknesses, and so on.

- An analysis of overall staff divided between employees and sub-contractors. Many companies employ sub-contractors in several areas; perhaps marketing, distribution, security and so on. Costs can often be cut by either making staff redundant and replacing them with sub-contractors or vice versa. Circumstances will dictate the best course of action.

- A detailed description of all the work that is sub-contracted, and profiles of the firms or individuals to whom the contracts have been given.

- The previous two years' accounts. This will give the consultants a reasonable financial profile of the recent history of the company. If there have been significant changes in the company in recent years then earlier accounts may also be useful in order to see how the company has reached the position it is in at the current time.

- Any available management accounts for the company. These will provide both a more up-to-date financial picture than the published accounts (which could be a year or more out of date) and also a more detailed analysis of the figures than is usual in published accounts, departmental breakdowns and so on.

- Cash flow forecasts. If these have been maintained over recent months then a comparison between 'forecast' and 'actual' should be available and will help to assess the accuracy of the company's predictions. Future predictions can then be assessed in that light, and in any case will provide some suggestion of the company's future expected situation.

- Any relevant ratios that the company uses to assess its financial health. These will vary from company to company but will usually include such basic ratios as gross profit (possibly divided between departments or products), staff to sales, profit to staff and so on. The consultants will want to calculate ratios of their own for various reasons; the information for these will come from the published and management accounts provided.

- Copies of the last two Management Letters from the company's auditors (in the case of limited companies). When conducting an audit the external accountants (auditors) will identify certain problems or deficiencies in the company's arrangements and will report on them to the company by way of the Management Letter. Clearly the opinion of external advisers to the company may be of use to your consultants.

- A list of your own problems to be dealt with. Every company has a few problems which may seem reasonably superficial and you and other directors will have a private list of actions to take. Often these will be the symptoms of deeper problems that the consultants will recognise. You may of course have seen the underlying problems in which case the material you bring with you will be all the more useful.

The action that the consultants will take when presented with the problem will vary from situation to situation. The first task is to identify the real problems, and these may not be what you think they are. The consultants will take time to analyse all of the above material, and more specific material that they will call for as the work progresses. However, swift action is usually needed to save a fast-deteriorating situation (in most cases) and so this should not be an overly prolonged affair.

The consultants will also be swift to act once you have agreed the matters to be dealt with. In a simple situation

of restricted cash flow in a large company they may cancel contracts for many company cars, sell the company yacht or plane, restrict over-generous expense allowances and so on, before moving on to more fundamental changes such as sale-and-lease-back of premises. The reason for this is not, as is often suggested, to look active but rather so that signals should be sent out to the staff and management of the company that changes are afoot. Once the whole company knows that something is happening it is easier to begin reaching agreement on what longer term actions are needed. These decisions may need to be worked through with the employees or their union representatives. Once agreement has been reached, then decisive and lasting action can be taken.

It may be that the company needs capital, the sources and varieties of capital are many; sales of shares, taking loans, seeking risk (venture) capital and so on. Your accountant will advise on whether capital is a solution, what sort is appropriate, and should also be able to assist in the preparations for raising such funds.

A word of warning: there are all too many consultancy companies who really have no experience of the work they set out to do and are virtually led by the directors, dealing only with the problems as presented by the directors rather than searching deeper for root causes and applying radical thinking to arrive at lasting solutions. This is often described as 'lend me your watch and I'll tell you the time'. (If you're really unlucky they'll sell you your watch back at a profit to themselves afterwards!) If your consultants seem to be acting in this way, confront them and – if applicable – change immediately. Consultants are most usually brought in when the position is already dire; an improper or inadequate approach on their part can quickly reach the point of being too late and the company is lost. (Then they will tell you the watch was already broken when you gave it to them!).

Briefcase Points

- Two years' accounts (more if there have been changes in recent years).
- Management accounts.
- Projected figures.
- Cash flow projections.
- Ratio analyses that have been undertaken by the company.
- Details of existing premises.
- Organisation chart together with CVs of key staff and all directors.
- Full summary of all employees.
- Details of work sub-contracted and profiles of all the firms to whom work is sub-contracted.
- The last two years' Management Letters from the auditors.
- A list of problems that the directors have already identified.

---

9 Assistance for meetings with a tax inspector

Generally speaking this particular situation applies to the self employed and those running small businesses. The Inland Revenue can ask any taxpayer to attend a meeting to discuss potentially underpaid tax, but usually the most complexity arises with the self employed.

We can assume that you have already prepared accounts of your business and have submitted them to the Inland Revenue. The inspector has written (to you or your accountant if you have one) saying that he is not yet able to accept the figures as he has questions arising from them. This is the beginning of an Inland Revenue investigation which is generally a thorough and searching enquiry that can last in excess of two years from start to finish.

The first stage, following the submission of your accounts, is that the inspector will request you to forward certain documents, including all the books and records of the business, possibly non-financial records such as diaries, copies of newspaper advertisements, and so on. He or she will go further and request all personal records, i.e. personal bank statements, savings accounts, dividend receipts and so on. There is no stated requirement for these records to have been kept in the way that business records must, yet the Inland Revenue will regard their failure to be kept as an offence in all but name; you are advised to keep these records along with business records as their absence may well be held against you. Such records will be demanded in respect of both you and your spouse.

It is interesting to note that since the introduction of independent taxation, where husbands and wives have their own tax returns and are able to keep their financial affairs confidential from each other, that the Inland Revenue apparently intend to ignore this point for the purpose of their investigations. One inspector I spoke to, who insisted on not being quoted by name, told me that he felt it would be all too easy for a husband or wife to switch assets to each other to hide them and that he would have to insist on both sets of records being presented to him. When I challenged this on the grounds that that would be directly against the spirit of independent taxation legislation he simply commented that there would always be a way round it; if he could not call for such papers then he would simply instigate a new investigation on the spouse and deal with it that way! In fact, Inland Revenue investigations – while usually conducted quite properly – are often one of the most unfortunate breaches of natural justice that a taxpayer can encounter. We shall come to this later.

Having received all of these various papers the inspector will then put together a financial picture of you and your spouse for at least one year. This will not only produce a profit figure which he believes to be correct but will also produce 'capital statements', i.e. an analysis of how your combined wealth has changed from the beginning of the year to the end of the year and whether or not that could reasonably have been funded from the profits or whether there appears to be a hidden source of income also involved.

After these statements have been prepared the inspector will ask you to attend a meeting. You should be under no illusion as to the position you are in. If you have an accountant then you are well advised to ask for him or her to attend the meeting with you. This is, in any case, logical since the accounts would have been prepared by the accountant who will be able to assist in answering detailed questions. If you have not had an accountant acting for you then certainly you should engage one for this purpose; just as a man charged with murder would not think to act without a solicitor, so you should not act without an accountant. You should not imagine for the slightest moment that you and the Inland Revenue are in some sort of partnership on this one. In fact, you should have engaged the accountant at the time you received the initial, enquiring letter from the inspector.

Since the major reason for needing an accountant in this situation is the position in which you find yourself with regard to the Inland Revenue, we should examine just what that position is. In my many years experience of dealing with investigations, the majority have at least been started (and indeed have been continued and conducted) on a fair basis with a quite proper determination by the inspector to satisfy him- or herself as to the correct position; but even in these best circumstances there is room for doubt as to the validity of the outcome.

The meeting with the inspector is designed to determine a position that is agreeable to both parties. To move to the end for a moment, when agreement on the year in question is reached then there are two stages that follow. Firstly, if the agreed add-backs to profit are substantial then the inspector will almost certainly exercise his or her right to make add-backs to previous years, based on that agreement. Precisely what is meant by 'based on' is subject to individual interpretation by inspectors, and the reasonableness of such add-backs varies accordingly. If you will not accept this then new investigations may be opened up on those earlier years.

Secondly, assuming that this agreement is reached, then the inspector will usually ask for an all-embracing settlement figure to be offered and paid, clearing up the matter in one go. The settlement will encompass tax deemed to have been underpaid, interest for late payment and penalties for the offence. Your accountant will seek to reach abatement of the penalties on the three grounds available: co-operation, disclosure and gravity of the offence. The inspector will also ask for a statement to be signed confirming that there are no other matters to be disclosed.

Most of the problems arise at the meeting where the 'underdeclarations' and agreements are discussed. It has been said that the Inland Revenue are seeking additional government funds to be made available for investigations on the basis that the vast majority (I was given a figure of 98 percent) result in additional tax being paid. This alone – on the face of it – would seem to justify the request. However, in a 'head-to-head' meeting between three district inspectors and many accountants the inspectors admitted that often the amount of extra tax paid was very small (I was involved with a client in one investigation that resulted in additional tax of £30 being paid after six months of analysis and correspsondence!).

It seems that the Inland Revenue may be more interested in the quantity of their successes rather than

the quality of them, presumably because of the guidelines they are under from the government to 'prove
their case'. At the meeting I mentioned above, it was
suggested that the Inland Revenue might even start
investigations for no other purpose than to increase
these numbers and that often very small add-backs
would be suggested which the taxpayer would find it
was easier and cheaper to accept than fight, so boosting
the numbers of successes. It must be said that all the
inspectors vigorously denied this suggestion, though it
was countered that – slightly to misquote Mandy Rice-
Davies – 'They would, wouldn't they?'

Motives aside, let us look at the position you are in.
Notwithstanding legal definitions, the practical position
is, frankly, that you are guilty unless you can prove
yourself innocent – and it's going to be pretty hard to
do that if you have the wrong inspector.

Let us suppose that all other matters have been
satisfactorily tied up, that all of the books and records
have been found to record all transactions, that the
income and expenses match the stated lifestyle of the
taxpayer. Then the inspector says, 'But I consider it
possible that you took £500 in cash for a job not declared
and then spent that cash on a weekend away somewhere in the country.' You try to prove you didn't! I
would agree that this simplified example is extreme, but
I have seen similar cases and heard of others; the
inspector is not obliged to prove his case, it is you who
are obliged to prove yours. It is difficult enough with an
accountant; I have nightmares about what must happen
to taxpayers who go it alone.

The following examples of situations that can arise
are all factual, though exceptional, and demonstrate
positions where the taxpayer would be very unwise to
go into the lion's den with nothing but his faith.

In one case I dealt with, the client had a very 'flash' car and the inspector made no secret of the fact that he took exception to it. After the meeting ended, at the end of the day, both the client and I saw the inspector getting on a bus (perhaps, for all we knew, to collect his Porsche from the garage!). Such prejudices actually only reflect the fact that inspectors are human after all.

Inspectors can also be obstinate; in another case of mine the inspector was unable to find anything at fault and in the end resorted to questioning the 'home as office' allowance. The claim made was £2 per week, which at the time was fairly typical of a claim made for one-man operations run from home. To be frank, this client was closer to living in an office than working from home to judge from his house, and his turnover of more than £100,000 showed he was certainly running no small operation. The challenge was really unwarranted and in this case I was glad to see the client obstinately refuse to be browbeaten and the inspector gave up the fight. One of the 2 per cent that got away!

The question of the inspector's competence must also be raised. I recall a case where I spent a long time explaining adjustments made in a set of accounts to an inspector who plainly did not believe me. (We eventually agreed that I was right.) I put it to him bluntly that I did not think he had the technical skills to prepare accounts and therefore could not be expected to understand them. He confirmed that he could not prepare accounts though he maintained that this did not prevent him from understanding them. I have some sympathy with the argument – I know how to operate a television set without being able to fix one – but I had little faith in this particular case.

The question of accurate records is also a curious one. The Inland Revenue maintain the position that if any – and I mean *any* – error arises in the records then they have the right to disregard *every* record's accuracy. There appears to be no question of materiality as there is in, say, company law. I suggested to an inspector that this would mean that the entire accounts of, say ICI, could be thrown out by the Inland Revenue if there was a one-penny discrepancy on the petty cash in one of that company's locations; the inspector stated that he held that to be true! It seems an unreasonable way of 'proving' a case; many more innocent people would have been hung than actually were if that argument could be used on evidence presented to courts. The Inland Revenue apparently does not have a provision for 'beyond reasonable doubt'.

The Inland Revenue's leaflet on investigations, IR72, states that the inspector will offer a reason for the investigation; in most cases that is true but there are times when doubts creep in. In one case, I dealt with a language school that took all of its pupils from contracts with schools in France and Belgium and in any case was full to capacity. The stated reason for the investigation was that there had been an increase in the numbers of students in that university town. True that may have been but it could have no bearing on the client, and the inspector must have known that.

Occasionally the inspectors get a bit out of order, for example using crude tricks against people. I was with a trader once who was explaining why his profits were low; he had bought the business in a rundown state and was seeking to woo back previously lost clients. The inspector asked him by how much he had put up prices in the last year and the client replied 'Between one and six pence per unit.' The inspector apparently sought to confirm: 'Did you say six pence?' and the client confirmed that he had. Adjustments were made to the

client's figures on the basis of six pence for *every* unit, which made a considerable (and quite incorrect) increase. The client challenged him 'I said between one and six pence.' The inspector replied 'I checked with you and you said six pence. I shall stand by your statement and if you want to argue with it you'll have to go to the Commissioners' (for appeal). When I put it to the inspector that he was not taking a fair line he simply replied 'I heard those words and I shall stand by them.'

I must point out that several of the examples I have given arise from one long investigation by perhaps the least competent individual I have ever encountered, though I also have to point out that I have collected stories from other accountants which are not mentioned here. So as not to lose a sense of proportion I stress again that the vast majority of investigations are conducted properly, indeed there have been several times when I think the inspector has gone out of his or her way to see things from the client's perspective. Those who have seen those hilarious scenes in the television programme *Minder* where the legendary 'Arfur Daley' and his accountant are explaining matters to the Inland Revenue cannot fail to have sympathy with inspectors.

Error is not all one-sided, either; I must be honest and admit perhaps the most embarrassing situation that has arisen for me in a meeting with an inspector. She was arguing the amount allowed in a set of accounts by a sole trader for his wife as assistant to the business. I explained all the duties the wife had to perform and claimed that £x per hour was not unreasonable. The inspector challenged me and suggested a lower figure. 'Where are you going to get anyone with reasonable common sense and anything like useful ability for less than £x per hour?' I asked. 'Well I earn less than that,' she said. (We got the amount allowed, and the investigation was a very fair one, by the way.)

A few practical points. The Inland Revenue inspector will make a written record of the interview between you, your accountant and the inspector. You are entitled to a copy of that record. The inspector may request that a second copy be signed by you to confirm your agreement with it. According to one inspector I

questioned they are not allowed to make a tape recording of that interview; certainly I have not seen this done
(or been certain that it has been at any rate).

If you or your accountant have any disagreement
with the way the investigation is being handled then
you can, in the first instance, ask for the District
Inspector to review the matter. I have found once or
twice that the threat of making that request has taken
some of the edge off less reasonable investigations
though I would imagine that the strength of the position would rely a good deal on the nature of the District
Inspector's relationship with the inspector concerned.

In the case of serious disagreement with the inspector
the taxpayer, usually through an agent, can ask for the
matter to go to the Commissioners. These are bodies of
non-Revenue people who adjudicate over investigations and it must be said that if the Commissioners err
on one side, it is often in favour of the taxpayer. Very
few of the many appeals listed ever go the the Commissioners, possibly because the Inland Revenue themselves seem reluctant for this course of action to occur.
Perhaps this point can best be illustrated by a technique
the Inland Revenue use to discourage would-be appel-
lants; if it looks as if you are seeking to go to the
Commissioners then you will be reminded that the
inspector has the power to reduce the penalties
charged, but that if you go to the Commissioners they
will seek *maximum* penalties. In short, accept what I say
or it will be the worse for you . . .

I would stress again that the point to be made in this
chapter, is that quality of inspectors varies. As in any
business there are a few rotten apples in the barrel; the
problem is that you don't get a sample to choose from,
you have to take the one you get. From the start of an

investigation then you are in the lap of the gods, and the necessary controls over the Inland Revenue that would provide reasonable justice appear to be slightly out of place if not missing altogether. Consequently, you need the professional assistance of an accountant.

Briefcase Points

- If you've got something to hide, its too late now. At least come clean with your accountant and so find the best way of presenting the facts.
- Examine your own living expenses and financial needs throughout the period that the investigation is covering. Make a written list of all your private expenses and go over this in detail with your accountant prior to the meeting. In the heat of the moment in the inspector's office you may forget important things; if you have noted them down over a period of a few weeks' thinking you will be better prepared to argue your case.
- Discuss the position with your spouse. (Every male taxpayer seems to forget about child benefit; with three children the household is receiving £1261 per annum at the time of writing – money you could be accused of concealing as income if you forget where it comes from!)
- When seeking to bridge a gap between your drawings (takings) from the business and your living expenses take time to think through the year in detail; there are sometimes exceptional items that get forgotten bearing in mind that the investigation might be looking at a period several

years ago. This could include cashing in insurance policies, sales of assets, inheritances, and so on.

- If you need to support an argument with documentation be sure to bring it with you to the meeting.
- If the inspector or your accountant have asked you to bring any documents to the meeting, seek them out in good time or risk having to have a further meeting.
- Discuss everything with your accountant in a pre-meeting and take his or her advice on how to conduct yourself. (You are in uncharted waters; your accountant has been there before).

10 Going for broke

Unfortunately, there may come a time when you need to see an accountant because you either are, or suspect that you are, becoming insolvent in which case there are certain special arrangements that need to be made. There are various forms of insolvency vehicles and it assists here to examine the various possibilities.

PERSONAL BANKRUPTCY

Individuals who have become insolvent, most of whom are commonly running their own businesses as sole trader or as part of a partnership (i.e. not an incorporated company business), become so when they can no longer meet their liabilities. Bankruptcy will occur either because the individual petitions to the local court, in effect walking in 'with hands up', or because a creditor to whom money is owed petitions to have the person declared bankrupt because of non-payment. A creditor may petition for bankruptcy if a debtor has failed to comply with a statutory demand made under section 268 of the Insolvency Act 1986 or if a judgment debt lodged against the person has not yet been satisfied.

COMPANY BANKRUPTCY

Members' voluntary liquidations

Not all liquidations are the result of doom and gloom. Occasionally a company may wish to cease trading and is able to pay off all its liabilities; alternatively the shareholders may wish to realise their investments. The directors/shareholders can place the company in members' voluntary liquidation which basically means that all of the liabilities are paid off and remaining assets realised to the owners.

Creditors' voluntary liquidation

When a company cannot meet its liabilities then the directors must take steps to place the company into a creditors' voluntary liquidation. This consists of the directors swearing a statement of affairs setting out the assets and liabilities of the company; this is then placed before the members and the creditors.

Compulsory liquidation

If a creditor has a judgment debt against a company, or the company has failed to respond to a statutory demand under the Insolvency Act 1986, then that creditor may petition for a compulsory winding up by the court. This will be dealt with by the Official Receiver (a government official) who will take the appropriate steps – usually convening a creditors' meeting.

Corporate voluntary arrangements

The Insolvency Act 1986 allows for a voluntary procedure to come into effect with the agreement of the creditors whereby a business continues running – either totally or in part – in an attempt to trade its way out of its difficulties. The majority of creditors must

agree to this otherwise the directors may be contraven-
ing the law by continuing to trade.

INSOLVENCY AND THE LAW

The particular circumstances which lead to liquidations
and bankruptcies have serious legal effects. If a director
continues to run a company in an insolvent state he
may face fines, disqualification and even a custodial
sentence under the Insolvency Act 1986. Therefore,
whenever the directors of a company, or an individual,
have reason to believe that they may be insolvent they
must seek advice as soon as possible in order to limit the
damage and to be seen to be acting in a responsible
manner.

The Insolvency Act 1986 (which came into force on
29th December 1986 along with the Company Directors
Disqualification Act) makes it an offence for anyone
other than an insolvency practitioner to administer a
liquidation or accept any insolvency appointments. It is
therefore important that the professional adviser you
approach is licensed under the Act to accept such
appointments. The regulatory bodies of the various
qualified accountants will be pleased to advise though
they cannot recommend individual people or firms.

In the case of most people facing bankruptcy, and
certainly in the case of companies facing liquidation, it
is almost certain that they will already have had accountants acting for them. In this instance it is therefore only
necessary to explain the current circumstances as best
as possible to the insolvency practitioner who can then
seek the appropriate documentation and information
from your previous accountants. This will be handed
over in the normal way under a clearance letter request.

(see Chapter 17, 'What happens when you change accountants'). Obviously the information you have to hand which makes you believe that you are likely to be insolvent should be taken to the meeting and will form the basis upon which advice is given by the insolvency practitioner. However, the majority of the information can be given by your previous accountants, relieving you of many problems at a time that will be full of other stresses.

Briefcase Points

- Previous sets of accounts.
- Current management accounts.
- Details of your accountants and auditors where applicable, together with details of solicitors and other advisers.
- Documents from creditors, the courts, etc. which relate to the current financial position.
- Any valuations of assets owned that may be affected by the action to be taken.

---

11 For those on PAYE who have tax queries

Generally speaking, the one group of people who have no need to engage accountants are those who have jobs which are taxed under the PAYE scheme and whose company accountants or personnel departments are available to interface between themselves and the Inland Revenue. In circumstances where there are limited allowances to be claimed and tax is payable at the basic rate there may well be no particular need for an accountant or for taxation advice.

However, even in these cases, and certainly in cases where there are exceptional allowances or higher-rate tax to pay, it is wise to take a 'health check' with an accountant to ensure that all available allowances are being claimed for and no excess tax is being paid. Such a meeting, if properly planned, can take as little as half an hour and involve a very minimum of costs.

Particular points which often get missed and need to be picked up specifically by the taxpayer, possibly with the help of an accountant, would be:

- Additional personal allowances in respect of unmarried people supporting children. These need to be claimed by ticking the appropriate box on

[97]

your tax return form but if the form is not received on a regular basis this can be missed.

- The married person's allowance for married couples. I have been surprised to discover that a number of my married clients were being taxed as single people before coming to me. Although they had been married for many years they had never made the appropriate claims. (Since the introduction of independent taxation this is now an 'additional personal allowance' rather than a specific 'married' provision).

- Higher-rate tax relief on mortgages. Mortage relief is given at the basic rate of tax and up until the 1991/92 financial year additional relief for those paying higher-rate tax was available but often had to be claimed for as it was omitted from the taxpayer's tax position. During 1991/92 higher-rate tax relief was abolished following the 1991 Budget.

- Many people who are provided with company cars or car fuel benefit are taxed at too high a rate because the appropriate rate has not been declared on their form P11D or indeed their company has not submitted it. Consequently their coding is severely restricted and too much tax can be paid. Form P11D is a declaration by a company of the benefits and expense payments given to its directors and higher paid employees.

- Often the taxpayer has not provided full details of, say, interest earned in building societies and banks where tax is deducted at the basic rate. The Inland Revenue raise estimated assessments for higher-rate tax which can be in excess of the proper figures but are often determined in the absence of any appeals or up-to-date information because the taxpayer simply does not know what to do with the assessment. Indeed, there are many times when taxpayers receive estimated assessments from the Inland Revenue and simply pay them believing them to be valid demands. There are many such occasions when an accountant can advise on the appropriate appeal and reduce this liability.

The possibilities are virtually limitless, but to prepare adequately for the meeting with the accountant it is advisable to go through your files and locate anything resembling the following.

Have at least the current, and possibly previous, year's form P60. This is the end-of-year summary of salary, income tax and National Insurance deductions provided by the employer for all employees after 5th April each year. This will provide the accountant with a clear picture of your major source of income. If your spouse is working, bring his or hers also, with their permission. If you have any forms P45 in respect of previous employment bring those to the meeting. This is even more important for those leaving employment; apart from supplying information that a P60 would provide if you had not left work it also gives the accountant a note of your most recent tax district and reference. Where no P60s or P45s are available then bring to the meeting payslips relating to the last year, or at least a sample thereof, so that the accountant will be able to put together some idea of your level of earnings in the recent past.

If you have any outstanding or recent correspondence with the Inland Revenue ensure that you have it with you. Also bring copies of your side of the correspondence. Many of the matters that the accountant will be able to assist in will have been noted by the Inland Revenue already who may well have written and are awaiting a reply. Often taxpayers fail to reply because they do not understand what is expected of them; the accountant can clear up some matters very quickly once the current state of play is known.

Bring any notices of assessment from the Inland Revenue. These are demands for tax and must be dealt with in a particular manner, within given time limits. They will also give an indication of the position as the Inland Revenue see it, which is a starting point for the accountant. The Inland Revenue issue notices of tax underpaid or overpaid on a yearly basis where necessary. Although they are not demands for payment, they indicate from where future demands, or repayments, may arise.

If you have received any 'notices of coding' from the Inland Revenue bring these to the meeting. They show how your tax code – the summary of your allowances – is made up and if there are errors in your current taxation it will often be reflected here. Common errors in such items as company car benefit are shown up by this document. Where there are any questions relating to car benefit or car fuel benefit bring details of the car provided by the employer; in particular the value when new, the age of the car and its engine size.

Have with you details of interest earned over the past year or more from interest-earning deposits. If possible bring the passbooks or statements relating to these accounts. Finally, as a general point bring any other documentation relating to specific requirements of your own.

As in all cases, it is imperative that before the meeting you are aware of precisely what outcome you want from

[100]

it. Even if you are only looking for a general review of your position there will be particular points that you want to cover. It is advisable in preparing for this sort of meeting to do more than simply review the position mentally; perhaps write out a list of the main points you wish to cover or the main questions you have. Not only does this make the meeting go more efficiently but it sometimes focuses your own thinking on to areas that either you had not thought to question or where the questions you need to ask are in fact more complex than you had first considered. By writing them down this becomes more apparent to you.

Briefcase Points

- Date of marriage if within the last six years or so.
- Your spouse's date of birth (and make a note of your own if you're prone to forget it!).
- Details of children, including birthdays.
- Copies of recent tax returns.
- Details of your mortage, preferably with statements from the lenders. Where applicable obtain a MIRAS 5 showing the interest paid.
- Details of your company car; particularly age, value when new and engine size.
- Copies of forms P11D submitted to the Inland Revenue by your employer. (You may have to ask your employer for these copies; they are not always given out.)
- Forms P60 for the past two years.
- Forms P45 where applicable.
- Recent payslips.

- Any correspondence with the Inland Revenue (their letters and copies of yours).
- Notices of assessment.
- Notices of tax underpaid or overpaid.
- Recent notices of coding.
- Details of interest earned (including statements and passbooks if applicable).
- A written list of any specific points you want to cover at the meeting.

12 Employing others

The many legislations and commonsense rules about employing others are the subject of several books of their own; it is a very complex subject. This is not the place for a detailed examination of this legislation, but we should look at the points to be considered before employing anyone. These are points that you can then discuss with your accountant, who should know your business well enough to help you make the important decisions.

Ensure that the job is necessary, and not one that can be done by reallocation of existing staff, training, sub-contracting or the introduction of technology. Having done that, decide where to obtain staff from: agencies, advertisements, search consultants ('headhunters'), etc.

If preparing an advertisement consider the legislation that covers employment law; discuss it with your accountant so that you are aware of your obligations. You cannot, for example, discriminate on grounds of race, sex, marital status or, in the case of Northern Ireland, where different legislation at present applies, religion. There are legal requirements in respect of contracts of employment too; discuss these with your accountant so that you do not fall foul of the law from the start.

Having obtained a member of staff, consider how best to develop and keep them; if you have not employed anyone before then your accountant can discuss with you such matters as training, motivation, assessment and promotion. If your accountant does not have this skill personally, he or she should certainly be associated with consultants who can advise. It may be that your business does not have a PAYE scheme opened with the Inland Revenue; your accountant can arrange this with the appropriate PAYE tax district.

Should the need arise to dismiss a member of staff, talk to your accountant before you do. There are many complex legislations which make it far too easy to fall foul of the law. Dismissal, even on the right grounds, can leave you open to claims for compensation if it is not properly dealt with.

There is also the moral question of how you deal with redundancy. Perhaps it is necessary to dismiss a member of staff because the job no longer exists; if so then there are constructive ways of doing so that do not hurt the staff member concerned. Explaining that it is the job that is redundant, not the person, is perhaps the obvious one. How you treat the staff you have to let go will be seen and remembered by those who stay on. There are specialist training courses available for companies to teach them how to deal with redundancy. These are a worthwhile investment for your company's future and your accountant can put you in touch with them.

The questions of whether to employ, who to employ and so on are too specific and too complex for any further discussion; but the message for the scope of this book is clear. Seek, and take note of, your accountant's advice and experience, and avoid the many pitfalls that a weight of legislation can offer.

Briefcase Points

- Details of the type of staff you require.
- Details of jobs needing to be filled.
- Job descriptions.
- Copies of proposed contracts of employment.
- Draft advertisements you have prepared.
- Copies of correspondence or written warnings given to members of staff that you are proposing to dismiss.
- Details of why certain staff may need to be made redundant.

---

13   Financial services

This chapter refers to financial advice regulated by the Financial Services Act 1986; it may be that you will seek that advice from your accountant or from another adviser. For the purposes of this chapter I refer to the rules formulated by the Institute of Chartered Accountants in England and Wales. However, most of the information applies whether your adviser is your accountant, or someone else. The chapter also assumes that your adviser has no knowledge of your financial picture; this allows for the maximum of preparation, and can be used if you choose to seek advice from a new source. Bear in mind, however, that your accountant may be the best person from whom to seek advice, as many of the necessary details are probably already on file.

FINANCIAL SERVICES LEGISLATION

The giving of financial advice is governed by the Financial Services Act 1986. It is fair to say that this was a much needed legislation to bring control into an area where poor advice, usually based on the adviser's own self-interest, was rife. Although members of the accountancy bodies were always regulated, if only by implication, there were many 'pirates' in the industry. However, it must also be said that introduction of the Financial Services Act has not been without its drawbacks. Apart from the technical problems of implementation and the financial difficulties caused to some regulating bodies there have also been serious effects on many accountancy practices, who once would have been typical financial advisers, but who have since taken themselves out of that market.

Undoubtedly the Financial Services Act has brought many benefits, but there have been difficulties too. Recent highly publicised disasters in the financial investment field which have left many people without their life savings show that the implementaion of the Act has not been totally successful. It seems analogous to the effects of the Tenancy and Rent Acts which were intended to give protection to tenants by strengthening their powers and weakening the rights of landlords; the intent was good but the result was to frighten away so many landlords that tenants were left not powerless, but homeless.

The Financial Services Act brought with it considerable costs in joining the regulatory bodies, which many advisers felt was improper in that they were effectively being asked to pay for rights they already had. It also brought with it considerable bureaucracy beyond the scope of some smaller organisations. As a result, many good financial advisers are now no longer acting in the field.

That said, the Act does offer some protection to those seeking financial advice. All financial advisers are authorised by some sort of regulating body. There is the SIB (Securities and Investments Board), various SROs

(Self Regulating Organisations) such as FIMBRA (Financial Intermediaries, Managers and Brokers' Regulatory Association), LAUTRO (Life Assurance and Unit Trust Regulatory Organisation), IMRO (Investment Management Regulatory Organisation), TSA (The Securities Association) and AFBD (Association of Futures Brokers and Dealers).

Accountants and solicitors are regulated by their own governing bodies who are RPBs (Recognised Professional Bodies) for the purposes of the Financial Services Act. Chartered accountants, for example, are therefore authorised and regulated by the Institute of Chartered Accountants.

When seeking advice from your accountant you should be given several documents, the two most important of which are probably the Buyer's Guide and the Letter of Engagement.

In the case of Chartered Accountants the Buyer's Guide is a one-page letter approved by the Institute of Chartered Accountants. It contains an explanation of the firm's independence, an outline of the Institute's Investment Business Regulations (which were agreed with the Securities and Investments Board) and details of what written information you may expect to receive about any financial products that you agree to buy.

The engagement letter sets out the instructions from you, as the client, that form the basis of your working relationship. It may be that the engagement letter you sign also instructs the accountants to act for you in other matters. Although usually quite lengthy, it is important that you go through this with your accountant and be sure that you are both in agreement with its terms.

FINDING THE FACTS

The basis of the Financial Services Act is that *best advice* must be given. This hinges on the principle of 'know your customer'. Therefore in order to make the best decision and, not unimportantly, to justify it to the regulatory inspectors, your accountant has to complete a 'know your customer' form (sometimes known as a data pack, fact-find, financial planning assessment, etc.). A typical form is reproduced at the end of this chapter. The questions asked allow for a complete financial picture and financial planning assessment to be made. The form also contains recommendations and a statement by you agreeing to, or modifying, those recommendations.

You must decide what you want and what you need and you can take advice towards clarifying this from your accountant. You will have an idea of what you see as your needs; your accountant may be able to identify other areas. For example, you may know that you need a pension but may not have identified a need for income protection; your accountant can determine this from the fact-find and advise accordingly.

Although the self employed, in particular, usually identify their need for a pension, your accountant may advise not starting a pension too early. The business will have other, perhaps more immediate, needs and your accountant will determine this and perhaps advise postponing a pension for a short period of time. With regard to pensions, they should be a target to aim for and not a random shot of just taking what comes. Your accountant will help to determine what your relevant financial position will be at retirement and what pension contribution is needed to maintain your required level of lifestyle.

If you are an employee then the accountant may decide to advise against index-linked policies. After all, what real relevance does the retail price index have on the salary of a person who might reasonably expect to be promoted, change jobs or career paths and therefore possibly increase their salary by considerable amounts? It is more useful to do a periodic review and reassessment of the position rather than relying on the random forces of inflation.

The fact-find will uncover your attitude to certain financial matters; details such as attitude towards life cover. Financial advisers suggest that in the United Kingdom life cover is generally much lower than it should be. The question you must ask of yourself is 'If I died yesterday what would my family's position be today?' or 'If my spouse died yesterday what would my family's position be today?' This also enables an estimate of the lump sum needed by the surviving spouse to be made and appropriate life cover to be taken out.

The fact-find is likely to be too complicated a document for you to complete alone unless you have some financial expertise. Therefore in preparing for a meeting with a financial adviser – be it an accountant or another independent or perhaps both – it is advisable to bring to the meeting all relevant documentation so that the information can be collated on the fact-find.

Such documentation would include:

- Your *bank statements* for the past year as these will contain details of existing direct debits and standing orders, the most frequent form of payment of insurances and pensions (it is surprising just how often once-a-year payments are forgotten when putting together details of insurances, etc.). The

[110]

bank statements will also give some idea of financial cash flow throughout the year.

- Any *existing pension policies*. Clearly to advise on what may be needed your accountant needs to know what exists already, and how flexible those policies are to new circumstances.
- Any *existing life assurance policies* for the same reason.
- Any *business-related insurances* such as key-man insurance, cross-policy insurance in respect of partnerships, key directors' income replacement policies, and so on.
- Documents relating to *previous company pension schemes*. If you have left employment or are moving from one employment to another, decisions have to be made as to what to do with the funds available. There are three courses of action available: leave the funds invested in the company scheme, transfer them to a new fund or move them to a personal pension plan. No best decision can be made until the transfer value of the fund has been calculated (and company pension fund trustees are notoriously slow in dealing with this question for ex-employees). Provided there are no time limits for action applicable to the situation, then delay is not always a bad thing; there are many legislations pending in the pensions industry which may make hasty decisions unwise. For example, the European Court of Justice appears to have ruled that all transfer values must be calculated on the basis of all men and women retiring at age 60, though there is some legal debate on this. There are also legislations to force all pensions to be increased by 5 per cent per year or the cost of living index, whichever is less. This would

affect transfer values. As an example, for a man aged 50 with 20 years' service behind him and currently earning £20,000 per annum the combined effect of these legislations could double the transfer value of his pension from around £30,000 to around £60,000.

Those who have moved or changed jobs or gone from employment to self-employment several times during their life can get a check from the Department of Social Security to determine the state of their pension entitlement. Retirement plans can then be made if the exact DSS position is known. An application to the DSS should be made ahead of time so that that information can be brought to the meeting. Difficulties in tracking down past pension benefits may be overcome by writing to the Pensions Registry; application forms are available from the Citizen's Advice Bureau.

AT THE MEETING

Generally speaking, any information should be collated which will be needed to answer the questions on the fact-find form but in particular ensure that you have details of any mortgage currently outstanding, salary, benefits in kind, investments and interest-earning deposits.

As part of the preparation for this meeting you are well advised to spend some time thinking about the questions on the fact-find. In particular, have a discussion with your partner or spouse to clarify in both your minds such areas as your priorities for what to do with surplus money, what your immediate needs are, and so on. Pre-planning for this kind of meeting is as much a case of establishing the position in your own mind as it is about collating documents and papers.

One further point. The Financial Services Act generally provides for a cooling-off period where there is a right to go back on decisions made at the time of the meeting. Be sure to establish at the meeting what that cooling-off period is and take the time to consider seriously if you have made the right decisions. If not, then notify the company that you have decided to change your mind and seek a further meeting. The decisions are yours to take and will affect you for the rest of your life; it is therefore important that you make the decision you deem most appropriate. You should never feel bullied or pressured into making decisions and any accountant that makes you feel that way should be dismissed without ceremony.

Financial advisers do not always get it all their own way. One independent adviser I spoke to told me the story of having three meetings with husband-and-wife clients to establish their priorities; the clients had not believed they had any surplus income but the adviser was able to show that with simple readjustments to their spending habits they had a certain sum available for other uses and he advised a programme of savings. Having established the investment pattern that they had agreed on the adviser then called back to finalise matters only to discover that the clients were so happy to have found surplus funds that they had taken out an HP agreement to re-carpet their entire house! Even in such circumstances a good financial adviser will wish them well and remain stoic and indeed will seek to maintain contact with them to advise them in future; he has plenty of time and space to cry in his own car later!

Briefcase Points

- Bank statements for the past year.
- Existing pension policies.
- Existing insurance policies.
- Policies covering existing business-related insurances.
- Details of present company pension schemes, including a valuation if available.
- DSS pension entitlement report.
- Details of mortage, including amount outstanding and monthly repayments.
- Details of current salary and benefits-in-kind received (such as company car).
- Past two years' accounts, where self-employed.
- Interest-earning accounts, including statements and passbooks where applicable.
- Details of investments held.
- Details of dependents.
- Date of birth of spouse (hopefully, you will already know your own!).
- Names and addresses of your other professional advisers.

Private and Confidential

Your Financial Planning Needs

This Questionnaire is designed to meet the 'Know Your Customer' and 'Best Advice' requirements of the Financial Services Act 1986.
Information will be treated in the strictest confidence. If you are unwilling to disclose information, the appropriate section will be marked **'non-disclosure'**.

Name:
Address:
Tel. No. Day: Eve: Date of appointment:
Introduced by:

A Personal Details

	Self	*Partner/Husband/Wife*
Title & Name:		
Marital status:		
Maiden name:		
Date of birth:		
Place of birth:		
Residence/Domicile:		
Smoker/Health:		
Occupation:		
	Full Time/Part Time/ Employed/ Self-Employed	Full Time/Part Time/ Employed/ Self-Employed

B Children/Dependants

Names and dates of birth	Current/future education/care costs:	Expected duration:
	£ p.a.	Years
	£ p.a.	Years
	£ p.a.	Years
	£ p.a.	Years

[116]

FINANCIAL SERVICES

C Home and Loan Details

Do you own your house?	Yes/No	Is the loan covered by Life Assurance?	Yes/No
Is it mortgaged?	Yes/No	Approximate value of	
In whose name(s) is the mortgage?		a) House	£
		b) Contents	£
What type of mortgage is it? Repayment/Endowment/ Pension		Do you own a second property?	Yes/No
		If yes please give details	
Date of commencement			
Over what term?		Do you have any other borrowings?	Yes/No
Who is the lender?			
		If yes please give details	
How much is the outstanding loan?	£		
Monthly net outlay?	£		

D Family Protection

	Self	Partner
Does your employer provide Death in Service benefit (lump sum and/or widow/widower's pension)?	Yes/No	Yes/No
If so how much?	£	£
What Life Assurance Schemes do you hold (including Income Protection)?		
Have you made out a will?	Yes/No	Yes/No
If yes, have your circumstances changed since you wrote it?	Yes/No	Yes/No
Do you periodically review your will?	Yes/No	Yes/No

E Retirement Provision

	Self	Partner
Does your employer provide a pension scheme?	Yes/No	Yes/No
If yes, what type of scheme is it (e.g. Final salary/Money Purchase)?		
How will your pension be calculated?		
Do you make contributions to your employer's scheme?	Yes/No £	Yes/No £
Do you make Additional Voluntary Contributions to provide pension benefits to supplement your employer's scheme?	Yes/No £	Yes/No £
Are you contracted out of SERPS?	Yes/No	Yes/No
Do you contribute to a personal pension plan?	Yes/No £	Yes/No £
Intended retirement age:		
Details of any other pension entitlements, e.g. deferred pensions/frozen pensions:		

[117]

HOW TO GET THE MOST OUT OF YOUR ACCOUNTANT

F Attitude to Investment   Are you: very cautious 1 2 3 4 speculative?(*circle 1, 2, 3 or 4*)

Current Values	Self £	Partner £	Capital Growth % p.a.	Income £ or % p.a.	Tax Net Gross Free
Main residence					
Current account					
Bank/BS deposits					
Shares					
Investment Bonds					
Unit Trusts					
Other property					

G Investments

Capital sums and other Securities held

Bank/Building Society £	
Unit Trust/Stock Exchange £	
Other investments £	
Others £	
Total £	

Identified short to long term expenditure

Sufficient cash liquidity retained?   Yes/No

H Personal Income   Self   Partner/Husband/Wife

	Self	Partner/Husband/Wife
Annual income before tax:		
– Earned	£	£
– Investment	£	£
– Benefits	£	£
Highest rate of tax paid:	%	%
How long will your income continue to be paid in the event of illness/disability?		
Do you have a financial services advisor? If yes, please give name and address?	Yes/No	Yes/No

[118]

FINANCIAL SERVICES

I Agreed financial objectives and priorities

Score each element: 1 = Most important 4 = Least important

1234	Income for your family in the event of your death, or the death of your partner	1234	Investment for children/ grandchildren*	1234	Make/review will: Inheritance Tax planning
1234	Greater tax efficiency	1234	Retirement provision	1234	Objectives of lump sum investments: capital growth/income/ balance*
1234	Provision for children's education expenses	1234	Capital provision for medium/long-term,* e.g. wedding for child	1234	Repayment of mortgage and loans
1234	Income for your family in the event of sickness or disability	1234	An emergency fund	1234	Others

* Delete where not applicable

J Other information

K Our Recommendations

To meet your requirement on the basis of information received, we recommend the following action:

We confirm that Terms of Business leaflet and Buyer's Guide have been left with the client

Signature	Date	Representative's name

L Your statement

I/We agree with the recommendations made and the enhancements to my/our financial plans
I/We prefer the following alternatives:
I/We acknowledge receipt of a copy of this form
Signature (self)   Date
Signature (partner)   Date (husband/wife)

[119]

14 Getting a mortgage

Mortgages are usually granted on the basis of a multiple of income and it would be fairly typical for a building society or other mortgage lender to lend three times the salary of an employee. This is apparently a rule of thumb which mortgage lenders find reasonably satisfactory though it has always been somewhat dubious since different people clearly have different calls on their net spendable incomes. However, there is rarely any reason for an employee to engage an accountant to assist in getting a mortage, removing it from the scope of this book. (As a point of interest though, recent house-market problems and mortgage repossessions have caused some building society chiefs to voice suggestions that in future the multiples may be reduced.)

For the self-employed the position is certainly less clear and sometimes somewhat more difficult. The same principles are employed by the mortgage lenders, i.e. a multiple of income, but the definition of income is far more difficult.

A typical set of self-employed accounts will have a turnover figure at the top of the profit and loss account – which may well be described as income – and

a significantly lower net profit figure available to the proprietor (before tax) at the bottom. This latter figure is really the equivalent of the gross pay of an employee. In the past, however, unscrupulous mortgage brokers have put pressure on accountants to verify income for this multiple purpose on the basis of the top figure on the profit and loss account, i.e. turnover. Supposing a person has a turnover of £30,000 and a net profit of £10,000; then £10,000 would be the gross pay equivalent and a multiple of three would provide for a mortgage of £30,000. However, if the lender can be persuaded that the person's income is £30,000 then a mortgage of £90,000 may be offered.

Not surprisingly mortgage lenders became very suspicious of this sort of attitude and now require completion of detailed certificates (or sight of the accounts themselves) in order to verify the position. The self-employed are usually asked for their accountant's details so that the accountant can write directly to confirm the position. (All that said, I know of at least one case of a nationally known building society who offered three times the turnover knowing full well what the overall position was. It was at a time when they were desperate to dish out mortgages; one of the most irresponsible offers I have ever seen but thankfully reasonably rare.)

Mortgage lenders will often ask to see the past three years' accounts to ensure that the current figures they are being offered are not a fluke. However, it may well be that the business has not been operating in its present form for that long. A mortgage is not impossible in these circumstances but the mortgage lender will rely heavily on the accountant to provide a projection of current and future earnings, which will not yet be on a set of accounts.

If self-employed, you are well advised to speak to your accountant to obtain advice as to what mortgage you can reasonably afford. This also gives your accountant a chance to obtain advance information relating to your current and likely future trading profitability. All too often I receive a demand for projected earnings from a building society at more or less the same time as a client telephones and says, 'Oh, by the way, I am going for a mortgage and you should be hearing from the building society soon.' It is then expected of the accountant to produce a reasonable projection of income by the next post, which is rarely realistic.

A bit of planning on your part enables the accountant to be well prepared for the enquiries from the building society or other mortgage lender and so able to respond quickly. Since there is usually a fairly fraught race at the point of mortgage offer and completion, this one part of the hectic hassle at least can be got out of the way ahead of time. Furthermore, you can be advised if you are seeking too high a mortgage for your means or too high a mortgage for your accounts to justify; this will save you from wasting a good deal of time and possibly money in pursuing the impossible.

It might also be noted that there are times when clients will approach accountants to ensure that the projection is 'favourable'. While there is certainly no reason why the accountant cannot view an uncertain position in the client's favour it is clearly inappropriate to expect the accountant to tell outright lies on a client's behalf. Optimism is one thing, deceit is quite another.

Less than scrupulous advisers will sometimes create more problems in getting mortgages than are necessary. Areas to look out for are as follows:

- Occasionally advisers will recommend cancelling existing insurances to take out new ones but this is in fact rarely necessary and if this is suggested, then the client should question this advice and be satisfied of the answers given.
- Some mortgage lenders impose hidden penalties such as a three-month interest penalty if the mortgage is to be moved, making it very costly to leave that particular lender. By 'hidden' it is true to say that the terms are included in the mortgage

document but usually with the same clarity that
one white grain of sand shows up on a beach!

- Some contracts have, say, a two-year, 2 per cent
  interest penalty for missed payments meaning
  that in the event of even the smallest missed
  payment a massive interest surge is put on to the
  mortgage for the next two years costing the bor-
  rower enormously. If this is coupled with a three-
  month interest penalty then moving the mortgage
  to avoid it becomes equally costly.
- Some companies have what amounts to a two-tier
  lending rate for different borrowers in the sense
  that there are fixed rates depending on when the
  mortgage is taken out. Knowing this position is
  simply a matter of studying the terms carefully
  and comparing them to other existing terms.

As with most things, you tend to get what you pay for
and often slightly more expensive-looking mortgages
may contain fewer pitfalls to be wary of – the clawbacks
of 'low-start' mortgages which can then suddenly become costly, for example. Another major point to consider is that changing mortgages should not force you to
keep going back to the start and taking out a new 25
year term. The better procedure might be to continue
the existing mortgage and take out only the new bit for
the new 25 year term. Generally speaking, this is less
costly in the long run and a more effective use of
endowment policies, where these are applicable.

Briefcase Points

A meeting may not be necessary, but as soon as you have decided to seek a mortgage be sure to telephone your accountant who can then prepare the information that will be asked for. If a meeting is necessary:

- Three years' accounts. (Your accountant should have these on file unless you have recently changed accountants.)
- Projection of earnings for the next 12 months, including some supporting documents (copies of invoices, details of contracts placed).
- Actual figures of sales for the period since the last accounts were prepared.
- Details of expenses relating to the above sales, if they are not in the same proportion as the previously prepared accounts.

15   Other tax and trust advice

The most common reasons for engaging an accountant
and tax adviser have been outlined in this book. In
addition there are many 'one-off' reasons which cannot
all be outlined, though the general points made, particularly in the Introduction, apply to all situations.
Certainly, if your circumstances are not run-of-the-mill
then the first step must be to telephone your accountant
and discuss the requirements of the meeting you are
seeking. Through discussion, the accountant will gain
some idea of what is expected, and can advise on the
items that you should prepare or bring with you. In
addition, the appropriate references or other material
that the accountant will need can be prepared in advance.

That said, there are three main situations which are
neither commonplace nor unique: the application of
Capital Gains Tax, the application of Inheritance Tax
and the taxation of trusts and estates. There are obviously aspects common to all three and these are noted
below as appropriate. However, these areas almost
always have unique or unexpected aspects to them, and
for that reason it is still suggested that a fairly detailed
telephone conversation be made when planning the

first meeting; it is simply not practical to list every possible situation.

In order that you can begin to prepare some basic material the skeletons of these situations are described below, with appropriate briefcase points.

CAPITAL GAINS TAX (CGT)

CGT is charged on chargeable gains (less allowable losses) that accrue to you on the disposal of assets during a given tax year. A chargeable gain is a gain arising after 6th April 1965 (the starting point) to any taxpayer (individual, company, trust etc.) resident in the UK, or in other circumstances on a non-resident trading in the UK. The particular assets that qualify also depend on the taxpayer's domicile. The precise rules covered here are complex which underlines the point that each taxpayer will have to present the pertinent facts to any accountant from whom advice is sought. For the purpose of this section we will examine the rules as applied to an individual; businesses, companies and trusts will already have advisers who will either be able to deal with queries on this subject, or obtain specialists who can.

Since 6th April 1988 CGT has been levied at the 'normal' income tax rate bands. Husbands and wives are treated separately. There are annual exemption limits below which no tax is payable. All of these points can be subject to review in each annual Budget, therefore no specific rates and amounts are given here.

The rule for CGT is that all assets are covered, with certain specific exemptions; these exemptions include private motor cars, your own home (main private residence), certain listed investments and assurance policies, gambling winnings, certain compensation payments, chattels (movable property such as chairs, paintings, etc.) sold for under a certain limit, and a host of less common items. A disposal for CGT purposes consists of more than just a sale; it can include destruction, gifts and surrender or sale of rights in an asset, though there are exemptions such as gifts to charity.

The computation of gains is complex, depending on the asset involved. If the disposal is of shares, then there are a multitude of regulations to wade through. However, none of this is of importance here since the computation will be done by your accountant after your meeting. Our task here is only to ensure that he or she has the right material to work from.

Briefcase Points

- Personal details of you, your spouse and (less commonly) anyone else involved in the transactions. This would include dates of birth and details of residence and domicile.
- Where applicable, e.g. if non-residency is to be established, dates of arrival in and departure from the UK.
- Details of the assets disposed of. In particular the date and cost of acquisition and the date and value of disposal.
- In the case of property, details of any improvement costs.
- Insurance or other valuations if applicable, or available.
- In the case of shares which may have been accumulated over a period of time, details of each acquisition, rights issue, etc. If you have a

broker they will be able to supply a history of the transactions they have dealt with on your behalf – bring this with you to the meeting.

- Due to a section of CGT legislation, it will be useful to have valuations of assets and shares at 31st March 1982. If you have such information to hand, bring this to the meeting.
- Any documentation pertaining to the asset, such as copies of insurance policies.
- The names and addresses of your other advisers, or previous advisers.

INHERITANCE TAX

Originally known as Capital Transfer Tax, this tax was renamed in 1986. It applies to lifetime gifts made after 26th March 1974, transfers on death after 12th March 1975 and settled property. Since 17th March 1986 most lifetime transfers are only subject to tax if death occurs within seven years of the transfer. The tax is raised on chargeable transfers; either on transfers you make or on your estate when you die. Since lifetime transfers escape tax unless you die within seven years, these are known as potentially exempt transfers (until you've survived long enough!).

If you are domiciled in the UK, or deemed to be by virtue of the Acts, then Inheritance Tax applies to all of your property, wherever it is. If not a UK domicile, then only UK property is involved. Inheritance tax is not so much a single event as a continuous train running from cradle to grave. Your accountant must therefore have a history, or maintain a history, of all your relevant transactions.

[129]

Briefcase Points

- A list of *all* current assets and liabilities. If assets have required a valuation, then copies of any such documents. This should include property, chattels, pensions and insurance policies. This list should be split between husband and wife.
- Dates of birth of both husband and wife.
- Copy(s) of any will(s) made out by husband and/or wife.
- A full list of gifts made in the last seven years, including the dates when they were made.
- A diagrammatic family tree including dates of birth and, where appropriate, dates of death.
- Where applicable, details relating to your domicile situation.
- Names and addresses of other professional advisers, or previous advisers.

TRUSTS AND ESTATES

A trust or settlement arises where one individual (the settlor) transfers assets to a trustee for the benefit of a third party (the beneficiary). On death, a trust can also be created under a will when an individual (the testator) sets aside part of, or all of, his or her estate which is to be administered by the trustees for the benefit of the beneficiaries. The administration period of the estate starts at the date of death of the testator and runs until the assets are distributed to the beneficiaries in accordance with the will or the rules relating to intestacy. Where the trust is set up by the will the administration period normally lasts only until the trust takes over the residue of the estate.

Your enquiry to your accountant may be because you wish to set up a trust or because you are a beneficiary seeking information about your own position. The briefcase points below will vary according to circumstance.

Briefcase Points

In the case of someone seeking to set up a trust, the same information will be required that is listed as Briefcase Points under 'Inheritance Tax' above.

In the case of someone seeking to understand their own position as beneficiary:

- A copy of the trust deed, which can be obtained from the trustees or executors.
- Any accounts of the trust to date.
- Names and addresses of trustees.
- Names and addresses of any other professional advisers, or previous advisers.
- Details of other beneficiaries (which should be noted on the trust deed).

---

16 If you have doubts about your present accountant

As a practising chartered accountant running a practice which has taken on many hundreds of clients pre- viously dealt with by others, I have heard many reasons why people seek to change accountants. Sometimes it is for purely practical reasons; changes in geographical location, going into partnership with someone who is already a client of the practice, and so on. However, probably the majority of the people recommended to me who are proposing to change accountants tell me it's because in some way they have doubts about their existing accountant.

Although some of these doubts are well justified many people have only a vague idea of why such doubts have arisen. Firstly, there may be disputes about fees where the client believes that the accountant is charging too much. I have to say that in many cases I privately, and silently, agree and am often proven right when we complete a subsequent year's accounts at a considerably lower charge based on similar records. However, no accountant is going to enter into a dispute over fees between a client and a former accountant and in many cases will insist that this is settled before taking on the assignment.

When transferring the client from one accountant to another the incoming accountant is required to request a 'clearance letter' from the outgoing accountant confirming that there are no professional reasons why he or she should not accept the appointment. The fact that there are fees outstanding is not in itself a reason for withholding professional clearance though the outgoing accountant may point out to the incoming one that fees are outstanding and certainly may hold books under a lien against settlement of outstanding debts.

Probably the second most common reason for people changing accountants is that they find their accountants slow to respond either to themselves or to enquiries from such bodies as the Inland Revenue. Sometimes this may be valid, but it may well not be all one-sided; clients often have very little appreciation of the Inland Revenue's own practices.

An accountant's office, if it is being properly run, must schedule its work. Quite often clients will send in their books and records without warning; these are therefore not on the schedule. Often this is acceptable to both the client and the accountant and time is given to schedule the work into the accountant's programme. In most cases the client trusts the accountant enough, and has a good enough working relationship, to say 'Do them when you are ready, but before they are urgently required.' An accountant who is well organized and aware of the needs of his or her client base then will be able to schedule the work according to priority.

Very occasionally, however, there are clients who will send in their records without warning and then phone up two or three days later to ask if the work is finished yet. They seem surprised when they are told that it may be a month or so before they will even be worked on

and will counter with comments such as 'But they will only take a day from start to finish.' Bearing in mind the natural clustering of year-ends around 30th April it would be conceivable for something like a quarter of the client base to send its books in during May, all expecting them back within a few days, which would clearly be impossible. This is why the accountants should be, and probably are, planning effectively.

So, bear in mind when you believe your accountant is being inefficient that it may be your own lack of planning that is causing it. More importantly, bear in mind that the problem will not go away by changing accountants since you will be taking it with you. Also remember that if you have priorities which are not already known to your accountant (e.g. you need the accounts because you need to present them somewhere), then be sure that you notify the accountant of those priorities beforehand. Most accountants will have enough flexibility in their planning to enable them to deal with a genuine emergency more quickly. Some will charge a premium rate as there is the possibility of having to take on additional temporary staff or diverting staff from other more lucrative work in order to meet your requirements.

Planning is a two-way street and the accountant cannot be blamed for the client's failure to assist in the process. By the same token the accountant must make clear to the client that such planning is required, and there are certainly some accountants who act on the principle of 'If it wasn't for the last-minute rush, nothing would ever get done around here!'

With regard to not being responsive to the Inland Revenue, clients who have enquiries underway with the Inland Revenue are often anxious about the outcome and will ring the accountant frequently to find out what is happening, it being very clearly the foremost concern in their minds. This is understandable, but it has to be appreciated that even a one-line letter to the Inland Revenue can sometimes take a month to generate a one-line answer (and not all Inland Revenue offices are that efficient!), so the accountant is powerless to force matters along at the speed which the client is requesting.

In other cases there are genuine reasons why negotiations between an accountant and the Inland Revenue are protracted; calling for and supplying other information and so on. These are probably not all understood by the client and there is therefore a tendency to blame outgoing accountants on the basis that 'These enquiries have been going on for months and nothing seems to happen.' In fact most enquiries go on for a good many months with long periods when nothing happens and about which there is very little that can be done.

Such a complaint does represent a problem between client and accountant, but it is a problem of communication between themselves. Clearly the accountant is not explaining to the client that these delays are normal and the client is failing to make clear such concerns to the accountant, who should then be able to allay them. If the accountant simply treats the client like a number and the client sits at home sweating in agitation but not speaking to the accountant, then clearly both parties are contributing to their difficulties.

Another reason given for doubting an accountant is that the Inland Revenue have instigated an investigation into your figures. In fact, accountants are rarely responsible for this. Generally speaking the Inland Revenue have information which suggests the figures are wrong and that is often because the client has not informed the accountant of a particular source of income, etc. Alternatively the figures may not fit the Inland Revenue's expected profile of results and they will question them on that basis; assuming that the figures have been correctly put together by the accountant then it is simply bad luck if the trading year has been abnormal and the Inland Revenue seek to look into it.

Occasionally there will be depresssed profits which have been compensated for by, say, the client taking out an extension to his mortgage. In those circumstances it is probably wise for the accountant to advise disclosing the additional mortgage as a specific point on the tax computations which accompany the accounts to the Inland Revenue. It may forestall enquiries and satisfy the Inland Revenue's questions ahead of an investigation. However, the Inland Revenue may still take the opportunity of undertaking an investigation and there is really very little that can be done to avoid that. Accountants must explain this position to clients to allay unnecessary suspicions.

Sometimes a client gets an idea that there is a difficulty between the accountant and the Inland Revenue when the Inland Revenue write directly to the client pointing out that they are not getting responses from the accountant. Perhaps so, but in many cases the client realises at this point that it is about time he answered the questions raised in letters from the accountants which have been piling up on the mantelpiece. Occasionally, however, it comes as a genuine surprise and may indeed represent a slackness on the accountant's part and therefore a genuine reason for having doubts.

Much more rarely, less-than-scrupulous Inspectors of Taxes (the Inland Revenue has its bad apples just the same as everywhere else) will attempt to use such a tactic to drive a wedge between accountant and client if the accountant – under instruction from the client – is sticking up strongly for the client's rights when submission might be regarded as the done thing. I have only encountered one or two such cases while speaking to other accountants but I do have one example of my own where my client received a letter from the tax inspector telling him that he was writing directly because he could not get a response from me. This, quite reasonably, resulted in an accusation from my client. In fact I was able to show him the correspondence file relating to the matter where almost every letter from the Inspector of Taxes concerned started with a phrase something like 'Thank you for your letter of such and such, and my apologies for the delay in replying . . . ' In fact I could demonstrate that all my responses had been appropriately timed and during the subsequent confrontation between Inspector of Taxes, client and myself (a normal part of the investigation procedure) the Inspector of Taxes 'withdrew any implied accusations' (they rarely apologize, but they do occasionally backtrack!).

Probably the least stated but actually one of the most common reasons for having doubts about your accountant is pure chemistry. If chemistry is the problem – and the fact is that some people simply do not get on – then recognise that it is not a subject for blame but simply a case of six of one and half-a-dozen of the other. Bow out of the relationship politely, and your accountant will probably be just as happy with the split as you are.

It may seem that this chapter is attempting to justify accountants' difficulties at the expense of their clients, but bear in mind that this book is designed to be read more by clients than accountants; clients already know their own difficulties and it is wise that they are aware of their accountant's problems in order that they can communicate effectively.

Briefcase Points

- Plan your work ahead of time with your accountant so that your needs are met, and the accountant's schedules are able to accommodate them.
- If you have urgent needs, make sure your accountant knows about them as soon as possible.
- If you have doubts, talk to your accountant about them. Most problems amount to a lack of communication and are easily solved.

17 What happens when you change accountants

One of the many apprehensions that would-be clients express is that of changing from one accountant to another. In fact it is extraordinarily simple with few significant consequences, yet it remains a major stumbling block for many.

Most people engage an accountant for the long term, expecting to use them again and again. In the case of those running businesses it is clear that there are advantages in using the same accountant year after year provided your working relationship is satisfactory. He or she will have some idea of your individual requirements, have a history of your business in their working papers and be familiar with the individual aspects of your particular bookkeeping system.

However, I have seen many cases where people have stayed with their accountants for many years after their working relationship has ceased to be satisfactory – in one case for over ten years – simply on the basis that they feared the consequences of change. Perhaps some of it is psychological, the devil you know being better than the devil you don't, but many have expressed their belief that it is a complicated legal procedure. In fact this is not the case and you have no ongoing commitment to engage an accountant beyond any existing assignment (the position with regard to engaging an auditor is different and covered in Chapter 3).

If the time comes to change accountants then you must first seek out and engage a replacement. Once you have satisfied yourself that a particular firm is suitable to take over your accounts then you will ask them to do so. This can be in writing or, in many cases, verbally. There is then the question of what you should do with

regard to your existing accountant. In theory you need not even contact them, but there are practical reasons why it may be sensible to do so. For one thing the incoming accountant will request confidential information and the outgoing accountants may well insist on having your written instruction that they should provide this.

Secondly, there is almost always some amount of unbilled work which the accountant has undertaken which will need to be invoiced. They will be reluctant to hand over papers which may be held under a lien (i.e. they have the right to retain papers against settlement of outstanding invoices) and it is as well to bring that situation to a head as early as possible.

Thirdly, and perhaps least significantly, there is a question of etiquette and style. In law there is no more need to explain to one accountant why you are not going to continue using them than there would be, say, to tell Woolworth's that you were planning to use Tesco's in future. In practice, however, there are differences; there is a relationship between client and accountant of a personal nature and it would certainly be extraordinarily impolite to engage another without first explaining the position to the outgoing accountant.

The new accountant, having received your instructions, will then write a letter of clearance to the previous accountant. This letter would typically be as shown on the opposite page:

Outgoing & Co.
Chartered Accountants
222 Park Road
Newtown
Berks.

1st April 19—

Dear Sirs,

A Client Esq
125 Bird Walk, Smalltown, Herts.

We understand that you act for the above. We have been invited to accept the appointment of their accountants and tax advisers and would be grateful to be informed if there are any professional reasons why we should not accept the appointment.

Assuming that there are no such reasons we would be grateful if you would supply us with the following:
1. A copy of the client's last tax return form.
2. A copy of the last accounts prepared for the client.
3. A copy of the last tax computations.
4. Any assessments, appeals etc. relating to the client.
5. Any books or papers belonging to the client.
6. Any other information of which you believe we should be aware.

We look forward to a reply at your earliest convenience.

Yours sincerely,

Incoming & Partners.

As you can see from the above the accountant requests 'clearance', i.e. that there are no professional reasons why he or she should not accept the appointments offered. This is very important to any accountant of professional standards. There may be cases where a client has gone to an accountant and asked for assistance in committing tax fraud by telling lies or preparing false accounts. If that accountant then refuses and the client seeks an accountant elsewhere then the outgoing accountant would have the right to explain the position to any successor, which would amount to withholding professional clearance. On the other hand the outgoing accountant cannot withhold professional clearance simply because of, say, unpaid invoices but, does have right to withhold some papers against settlement.

Once clearance has been given the outgoing accountant will provide the information requested above. The new accountant will then obtain a form 64–8; this is an authority form on the Inland Revenue's own notepaper which enables the Inland Revenue to send details of confidential information to the accountant. This form automatically supersedes any previous form (i.e. it invalidates the 64–8 of the previous accountants). From that point on the Inland Revenue will correspond with the new accountants who will have all the information necessary to take over.

Very importantly, the accountant – whether you are changing to a new accountant or starting with your first – will require the completion of a Letter of Engagement. This sets out the working relationship between you. Examine this letter and be sure that you agree with its terms.

As you can see there is nothing more than the slightest correspondence on the part of the client and in most cases a minimum of fuss between the two accountants in changing over. There may be cases where no replies are received to letters sent in which case the incoming accountant simply makes a decision to take over and requests the required information directly from the Inland Revenue. Once information is received from both the Inland Revenue and the client themselves, the changeover is not difficult. To cover the situation regarding professional clearance the accountants can issue a registered letter to the outgoing accountants who have not replied, simply stating that they will be taking over the position unless a reply is received within a certain time period.

To summarise, the procedure is simple: once a replacement accountant has been chosen it only needs a letter from you to the outgoing accountant, minor correspondence between the accountants, the signing of a couple of forms, and the new client/accountant relationship is able to proceed. The Briefcase Points below will be required for your first visit to your new accountant.

Briefcase Points

- Your previous accountant's name, address and telephone number.
- A copy of your last accounts (the new accountant will need to get some idea of the scope of the business).
- As many details of your business as possible. (Use the various briefcase points in the other sections of this book as a guideline.)
- Details of any urgent, or outstanding, matters that require attention.

Index

Accountants, ix, x, xi, xiii, 1–3,
  5–16, 19–24, 26–31, 33, 38, 43,
  45, 50–3, 55–9, 63, 65–7, 70–4,
  79, 83–5, 89, 91–3, 95–7,
  99–100, 103–4, 106, 108–10,
  113, 120–3, 125–6, 129,
  131–42, 144–5
Accountant's audit charge, xi,
  9, 12, 44–5, 49, 63–4, 132
Accounting Technician, 3
Accounts, 7, 39–40, 42, 45,
  55–7, 59–60, 73, 76, 80, 86,
  96, 115, 120, 122–3, 125, 131,
  141, 143–5
'Acid test', 61
Acquisition, 54
Additional personal allowance,
  97
AFBD, 108
All risks insurance, 35
Annual accounting scheme, 24
Appeals (against tax
  assessment), 88, 143
Assessments, 15, 19–21, 98–9,
  100, 102, 143
Audit(or), 43–9, 77, 80, 96, 141
Audit report, 4, 9–10, 39–40,
  42–3, 45–7, 57, 67
Auditing standards, 41

Bad debts, 61
Badges of self-employment, 18
Badges of trade, 16
Badwill, 58
Balance sheet, 29, 57
Bank, 12, 14, 39, 43, 45, 52, 57,
  60, 63, 67
Bankruptcy, 93–5
Beneficiary, 131
Book-keeping/Book-keepers, 4,
  8, 23–4, 30–1, 41, 45, 140
Briefcase points, xiii, 9, 12, 14,
  20, 22, 25, 28, 31, 33, 38, 49,
  54, 64, 68, 73, 80, 91, 96, 101,
  105, 115, 125, 128, 130–1, 139,
  145
Building industry, 8, 19
Building society, 120, 122–3
Business interruption
  insurance, 36
Business plan, 6, 11–12, 14, 30
'Buyers guide', 108

Capital Allowances, 20

Capital expenditures, 27
Capital Gains Tax, 5, 27, 32–3, 126–9, 128, 129
Capital (introduced), 29
Capital Statements, 82
Capone, Al, 25
Cash Accounting Scheme (for VAT), 24
Cash book, 30
Cash flow (forecast), 13–14, 76, 79–80
Certified Accountants, 3–4, 41, 43
Charities, 49, 128
Chartered Accountants, 3, 7–8, 41, 43, 108
Cheque (stubs), 30
Citizens Advice Bureau, 112
Class 1 National Insurance contributions, 21–2
Class 2/Class 4 National Insurance contributions, 21–2
Close company status, 53
Code (PAYE), 100, 102
Commissioners (of the Inland Revenue), 88, 90
Companies Acts, x, 4, 11, 39, 41, 43, 45, 68
Companies House, 63
Company cars, 58, 98, 100–1, 115
Company Directors Disqualification Act, 95
Compensation for loss of office, 94
Compulsory liquidation, 84
Computer, 28, 30–1
Consultants, 74–9, 104
Copyrights, 59
Corporate voluntary arrangements, 94

Covenant, 59
Credit terms, 13, 15
Creditors, 39, 43, 45, 52, 61, 94
Creditors voluntary liquidation, 94
Current assets, 60–1
Current liabilities, 60–1
Current ratio, 60
Customs and Excise, 23
CV, 13–14, 64, 76, 80

Daley, Arthur, 89
Debts/Debtors, 29–30, 39, 45, 60
Deferment (for National Insurance contributions), 21
Department of Social Security, 21, 112, 115
Department of Trade, 4, 43, 49
Directors, 11, 14, 42–3, 47, 49–51, 64–6, 75, 77, 79–80, 94–5, 98
Dismissal (of staff), 104
District Inspector (of Inland Revenue), 90
Dividends, 54
Domestic insurance, 33, 35
Double entry book-keeping, 4
Drawings, 28

Employees Liability Insurance, 34, 37
Employees (staff), 13–14, 22, 70, 76, 79–80, 98, 103, 110
Entertainment industry, 81
Equipment (fixed assets), 15, 26, 28, 31, 56, 64
Executors, 131
Exemption (for N.I. contributions), 21
Expenses, 28, 31, 125

Family tree, 130
Film industry, 8, 19
FIMBRA, 108
Finance, 14
Financial planning, 5
Financial services, 106
Financial Services Act 1986, 106–9, 113
Fixed assets, 56
41G (form), 19
Franchising, 69–71, 73

'Going public', 53–4
Goods in transit insurance, 34
Goodwill, 58–9, 67
Government schemes, 14
Gross profit, 62, 77

Higher rate (of tax), 97–8
Historical cost convention, 41
'Hostile' takeover bid, 48

IMRO, 108
Income, 11, 20, 28, 59, 73, 83
Income protection insurance, 36, 109
Incorporation, 11
Inheritance tax, 5, 126, 129, 131
Inland Revenue, 4–8, 15–22, 26, 33, 59–60, 81–5, 87, 89–91, 96, 98–102, 104, 133, 135–7, 144–5
Insolvency, 61, 95–6
Insolvency Act 1986, 93–5
Insolvency practitioner, 95
Inspector of Taxes, 19, 81–90, 92, 137, 138
Institute of Cost and Management Accountants, 3
Institutes of Chartered Accountants, 3–4, 41, 106, 108

Insurances, 33–4, 37–8, 111, 115, 123
Interest charges (tax), 6, 19, 84
Interest (earned), 57, 100, 102
'Introduction' (to Stock Exchange), 53
Investigation (Inland Revenue), 6–7, 82–3, 85, 87, 89–91, 136–8
Invoices, 28–9, 46, 67, 142, 144
IR72 (leaflet), 87

Job descriptions, 105
Journals, 30

Key personnel, 13, 46, 64, 66, 76, 80

LAUTRO, 108
Leasing, 31, 33, 64, 75
Letter of clearance, 142–4
Letter of engagement, 108, 144
Lien, 142
Life insurance, 38, 111
Limited Company, 4–5, 9, 11, 39, 63, 69, 77
Liquidation, 94–5
Local authorities, 32

Machinery, 13
Management accounts, 13–14, 55, 57, 60, 64, 67, 76–7, 80, 96
Management 'buy-out', 53
Management consultancy, 50–2, 74
Management letters, 77, 80
Market research, 13, 15, 69
Marx, Groucho, 24
Members voluntary liquidation, 94
Merger, 54

'Minder' (TV programme), 89
MIRAS, 5, 101
Mortgages, 98, 115, 120, 122–5, 136–7
Motor insurance, 35

National insurance, 20–2, 99
Net profit, 62, 121
Nominal ledger, 30
Notice of coding (PAYE), 100

'Offer for sale', 53
Office contents insurance, 35
Official receiver, 94
Opening/Closing year rules (for tax), 15
Organisation chart, 75, 80
Outside the scope (of VAT), 26
Overheads, 62

Partnerships, 5, 11, 14–15, 69, 132
PAYE (pay as you earn), 16, 29, 97, 104
P11D (form), 98, 101
Penalties (Inland Revenue), 6, 19, 23, 84
Pensions, 37–8, 109, 111, 115
Pensions registry, 112
Personal allowances, 20
Personal information, 19
Petty Cash Book, 30
P45 (form), 20, 22, 99, 101
'Placing', 53
Planning permission, 32
Premises, 13, 15, 28, 31–2, 44, 56, 64, 75, 80
Pricing policy, 13–15
Private Health Insurance, 36
Products liability insurance, 34
Profit and loss account, 120

Profit forecast, 13–15
Profits, 15, 17, 22, 27, 59, 62, 67–8, 71, 83, 87, 136
Property insurance, 35
Proprietor, 63, 67
Projected accounts, 55, 64, 73, 80
P60 (form), 99, 101
Public liability insurance, 34
Purchase Day Books, 29–30
Purchase Ledger, 29–30
Pyramid selling, 70

Qualified accountants, 3–4, 7–9, 39

Ratios, 60, 62, 77, 86
Recommendation, 9, 44
Records (of transactions), 28–31, 44–6, 49
Redundancy, 66, 76, 104
Residency (for tax), 32
Revenue expenditure, 27
Rice-Davies, Mandy, 85
Royal Commission (1954), 16
Royalties (franchise), 70
Ruthledge v The Commissioners of the Inland Revenue (1929), 16

'Sale and lease back', 75, 79
Sales Day Book, 28, 30
Sales ledger, 28, 30
Schedule D, 16
Securities and Investment Board (SIB), 107
Self-employment, 10–11, 15–19, 21–3, 26, 36–9, 66, 70, 81, 109, 120, 122
Self-regulating organisations (SRO), 107–8

INDEX

Service contracts (directors), 64, 66
Share issues, 54
Shareholders, 11, 42–3, 52–4, 65, 94,
64–8 (form), 19–21, 144
Social/Domestic/Pleasure Motor Insurance, 35
Software, 30
Solicitors, ix, xiii, 33, 49, 51, 59, 70–1, 96
Source and application of funds, 41
Standard-rated (for VAT), 26
Stock market, 53–4
Stocks, 29, 57, 60, 64
Sub-contractors, 64, 76, 80, 103
Systems audit, 39, 46

Takeovers, 54
Tax computations, 137, 143
Tax payer, 21, 81, 85
Tax rates, 20
Tax reference, 20
Tax return form, 19, 143
Taxation, 10, 22, 84, 100, 102
Taxes Act, x, 16
Tenancy, 33
Testator, 130
Time limits, 6, 19
Trademarks, 59

Trading, 14, 16–17, 31, 64
Training, 70, 103, 104
'True and fair view', 41
Trusts, 126, 130
TSA, 108
Turnover, 23, 25, 29, 59, 67, 70, 120–1

Unemployment Benefit Office, 20, 22
Unqualified accountants, 3–4, 7–9

Valuations, 56–7
VAT (Value Added Tax), 22–5
VAT returns, 24
Voluntary liquidation, 94
Voluntary registration (for VAT), 23, 25

Wages, 29, 31
Work-in-progress, 57, 60, 64
Working capital, 57
Working from home, 6, 27, 32–5
Written down value, 27

Year end, 6, 15, 29, 41

Zero-rated (for VAT), 26